Basic and Clinical Science Course
Section 10

Glaucoma

1999-2000

(Last major revision 1996-1997)

LEO

LIFELONG

EDUCATION FOR THE

OPHTHALMOLOGIST

American Academy of Ophthalmology

The Basic and Clinical Science Course is one component of the Lifelong Education for the Ophthalmologist (LEO) framework, which assists members in planning their continuing medical education. LEO includes an array of clinical education products that members may select to form individualized, self-directed learning plans for updating their clinical knowledge. Active members or fellows who use LEO components may accumulate sufficient CME credits to earn the LEO Award. Contact the Academy's Clinical Education Division for further information on LEO.

This CME activity was planned and produced in accordance with the ACCME Essentials.

The Academy provides this material for educational purposes only. It is not intended to represent the only or best method or procedure in every case, nor to replace a physician's own judgment or give specific advice for case management. Including all indications, contraindications, side effects, and alternative agents for each drug or treatment is beyond the scope of this material. All information and recommendations should be verified, prior to use, with current information included in the manufacturers' package inserts or other independent sources, and considered in light of the patient's condition and history. Reference to certain drugs, instruments, and other products in this publication is made for illustrative purposes only and is not intended to constitute an endorsement of such. Some material may include information on applications that are not considered community standard, that reflect indications not included in approved FDA labeling, or that are approved for use only in restricted research settings. The FDA has stated that it is the responsibility of the physician to determine the FDA status of each drug or device he or she wishes to use, and to use them with appropriate patient consent in compliance with applicable law. The Academy specifically disclaims any and all liability for injury or other damages of any kind, from negligence or otherwise, for any and all claims that may arise from the use of any recommendations or other information contained herein.

Basic and Clinical Science Course

Thomas A. Weingeist, PhD, MD, Iowa City, Iowa
Senior Secretary for Clinical Education

Thomas J. Liesegang, MD, Jacksonville, Florida
Secretary for Instruction

M. Gilbert Grand, MD, St. Louis, Missouri
BCSC Course Chair

Section 10

Faculty Responsible for This Edition

Louis Cantor, MD, *Chair,* Indianapolis, Indiana

Michael S. Berlin, MD, Los Angeles, California

Elizabeth A. Hodapp, MD, Miami, Florida

David A. Lee, MD, Los Angeles, California

M. Roy Wilson, MD, Los Angeles, California

Martin Wand, MD, Hartford, Connecticut
Practicing Ophthalmologists Advisory Committee for Education

Recent Past Faculty

A. Robert Bellows, MD

Frank G. Berson, MD

Michael A. Kass, MD

Stephen B. Lichtenstein, MD

Bradford J. Shingleton, MD

Robert L. Stamper, MD

Richard Stone, MD

In addition, the Academy gratefully acknowledges the contributions of numerous past faculty and advisory committee members who have played an important role in the development of previous editions of the Basic and Clinical Science Course.

American Academy of Ophthalmology Staff

Kathryn A. Hecht, EdD
Vice President, Clinical Education

Hal Straus
Director, Publications Department

Margaret Denny
Managing Editor

Fran Taylor
Medical Editor

Maxine Garrett
Administrative Coordinator

American Academy of Ophthalmology
655 Beach Street
Box 7424
San Francisco, CA 94120-7424

CONTENTS

PAGE

General Introduction ix
Objectives for BCSC Section 10 1
Introduction to Section 10 3
Historical Introduction: Development of Our Concept of Glaucoma 5

I. Introduction and Definitions 7

II. Social and Economic Aspects of Glaucoma 9

III. Hereditary and Genetic Factors 10

IV. Classification 11

V. Intraocular Pressure and Aqueous Humor Dynamics 14

  Aqueous humor formation 14
  Aqueous humor outflow 16
    Trabecular outflow 16
    Uveoscleral outflow 16
    Tonography 17
  Episcleral venous pressure 18
  Intraocular pressure 18
    Distribution in the population and relation to glaucoma 18
    Factors influencing intraocular pressure 19
    Diurnal variation 19
    Clinical measurement of intraocular pressure 19
    Infection control in clinical tonometry 24

VI. Clinical Evaluation 25

  History and general examination 25
    History 25
    Refraction 25
    Pupils 25
    Biomicroscopy 26
    Other tests 26
  Gonioscopy 27
  The optic nerve 36
    Anatomy and pathology 36
    Theories of glaucomatous damage 40
    Examination of the optic nerve head 40
    Clinical evaluation of the optic nerve head 41

Recording of optic nerve findings 44
The visual field 44
    Clinical perimetry 46
    Patterns of glaucomatous nerve loss 47
    Variables in perimetry 47
    Manual perimetry 53
    Automated static perimetry 55
    Test types and applications 56
    Interpretation of a single field 57
    Interpretation of a series of fields 60

VII. Open-Angle Glaucoma 66

Primary open-angle glaucoma 66
    Epidemiology 66
    Genetics 66
    Clinical features 67
    Associated disorders 67
The glaucoma suspect 68
Normal- (low-) tension glaucoma 69
    Clinical features 70
    Differentail diagnosis 70
    Diagnostic evaluation 71
    Prognosis and therapy 72
Secondary open-angle glaucoma 72
    Exfoliation syndrome (pseudoexfoliation) 72
    Pigmentary glaucoma 74
    Lens-induced glaucoma 76
    Intraocular tumors 76
    Ocular inflammation and secondary open-angle glaucoma 76
    Raised episcleral venous pressure 77
    Accidental and surgical trauma 77
    Drugs and glaucoma 80

VIII. Angle-Closure Glaucoma 81

Mechanisms and pathophysiology of angle closure 81
Primary angle-closure glaucoma with pupillary block 82
    Epidemiology 82
    Pathophysiology 83
    Acute primary angle-closure glaucoma 83
    Subacute angle-closure glaucoma 84
    Chronic angle-closure glaucoma 85
    Provocative tests for angle closure 85
Primary angle-closure glaucoma without pupillary block 86
Secondary angle-closure glaucoma with pupillary block 88
    Lens-induced angle-closure glaucoma 88

Secondary angle-closure glaucoma without pupillary block 89
    Previous pupillary block 89
    Flat anterior chamber 89
    Neovascular glaucoma 90
    Iridocorneal endothelial (ICE) syndrome 91
    Tumors 91
    Inflammation 93
    Ciliary-block glaucoma 93
    Epithelial and fibrous downgrowth 94
    Trauma 94
    Retinal surgery and retinal vascular disease 94
    Nanophthalmos 95
    Fuchs corneal endothelial dystrophy 95
    Retinopathy of prematurity 95

IX. Combined-Mechanism Glaucoma 96

X. Childhood Glaucoma 97

    Definitions and classification 97
    Epidemiology and genetics 97
    Clinical features 98
    Pathophysiology 99
    Differential diagnosis 99
    Long-term prognosis and follow-up 100
    Developmental glaucomas with associated anomalies 101

XI. Medical Management of Glaucoma 104

    Medical agents 105
    Beta-adreneric antagonists (beta blockers) 105
    Adrenergic agonists 106
    Parasympathomimetic agents 106
    Carbonic anhydrase inhibitors (CAIs) 111
    Prostaglandin analogs 111
    Hyperosmotic agents 112
    General approach to medical treatment 112
    Open-angle glaucoma 112
    Angle-closure glaucoma 113

XII. Surgical Therapy of Glaucoma 114

    Open-angle glaucoma 114
    Laser surgery 116
    Incisional surgery 118
    Other procedures (incisional and nonincisional) 122
    Angle-closure glaucoma 123
    Laser surgery 123
    Incisional surgery 125
    Childhood glaucoma 125
    Incisional surgery 125
    Laser surgery 126

XIII. Low-Vision Aids in Glaucoma Patients 128

   Evaluation of low-vision patients with glaucoma 128
      Management 129

Basic Texts 130
Related Academy Materials 131
Credit Reporting Form 133
Study Questions 135
Answers 141
Index 144

GENERAL INTRODUCTION

The Basic and Clinical Science Course (BCSC) is designed to provide residents and practitioners with a comprehensive yet concise curriculum of the field of ophthalmology. The BCSC has developed from its original brief outline format, which relied heavily on outside readings, to a more convenient and educationally useful self-contained text. The Academy regularly updates and revises the course, with the goals of integrating the basic science and clinical practice of ophthalmology and of keeping current with new developments in the various subspecialties.

The BCSC incorporates the effort and expertise of more than 70 ophthalmologists, organized into 12 section faculties, working with Academy editorial staff. In addition, the course continues to benefit from many lasting contributions made by the faculties of previous editions. Members of the Academy's Practicing Ophthalmologists Advisory Committee for Education serve on each faculty and, as a group, review every volume before and after major revisions.

Organization of the Course

The 12 sections of the Basic and Clinical Science Course are numbered as follows to reflect a logical order of study, proceeding from fundamental subjects to anatomic subdivisions:

1. Update on General Medicine
2. Fundamentals and Principles of Ophthalmology
3. Optics, Refraction, and Contact Lenses
4. Ophthalmic Pathology and Intraocular Tumors
5. Neuro-Ophthalmology
6. Pediatric Ophthalmology and Strabismus
7. Orbit, Eyelids, and Lacrimal System
8. External Disease and Cornea
9. Intraocular Inflammation and Uveitis
10. Glaucoma
11. Lens and Cataract
12. Retina and Vitreous

In addition, a comprehensive Master Index allows the reader to easily locate subjects throughout the entire series.

References

Readers who wish to explore specific topics in greater detail may consult the journal references cited within each chapter and the Basic Texts listed at the back of the book. These references are intended to be selective rather than exhaustive, chosen by the BCSC faculty as being important, current, and readily available to residents and practitioners.

Related Academy educational materials are also listed in the appropriate sections. They include books, audiovisual materials, self-assessment programs, clinical modules, and interactive programs.

Study Questions and CME Credit

Each volume includes multiple-choice study questions designed to be used as a closed-book exercise. The answers are accompanied by explanations to enhance the learning experience. Completing the study questions allows readers both to test their understanding of the material and to demonstrate section completion for the purpose of CME credit, if desired.

The Academy is accredited by the Accreditation Council for Continuing Medical Education to sponsor continuing medical education for physicians. CME credit hours in Category 1 of the Physician's Recognition Award of the AMA may be earned for completing the study of any section of the BCSC. The Academy designates the number of credit hours for each section based upon the scope and complexity of the material covered (see the Credit Reporting Form in each individual section for the maximum number of hours that may be claimed).

Based upon return of the Credit Reporting Form at the back of each book, the Academy will maintain a record, for up to 3 years, of credits earned by Academy members. Upon request, the Academy will send a transcript of credits earned.

Conclusion

The Basic and Clinical Science Course has expanded greatly over the years, with the addition of much new text and numerous illustrations. Recent editions have sought to place a greater emphasis on clinical applicability, while maintaining a solid foundation in basic science. As with any educational program, it reflects the experience of its authors. As its faculties change and as medicine progresses, new viewpoints are always emerging on controversial subjects and techniques. Not all alternate approaches can be included in this series; as with any educational endeavor, the learner should seek additional sources, including such carefully balanced opinions as the Academy's Preferred Practice Patterns.

The BCSC faculty and staff are continuously striving to improve the educational usefulness of the course; you, the reader, can contribute to this ongoing process. If you have any suggestions or questions about the series, please do not hesitate to contact the faculty or the managing editor.

The authors, editors, and reviewers hope that your study of the BCSC will be of lasting value and that each section will serve as a practical resource for quality patient care.

OBJECTIVES FOR BCSC SECTION 10

Upon completion of BCSC Section 10, *Glaucoma,* the reader should be able to:

□ Identify the epidemiological features of glaucoma, including the social and economic impacts of the disease

□ Summarize recent advances in the understanding of hereditary and genetic factors in glaucoma

□ Outline the physiology of aqueous humor dynamics and the control of intraocular pressure

□ Review the clinical evaluation of the glaucoma patient, including history and general examination, gonioscopy, optic nerve examination, and visual field

□ Describe the clinical features of the patient considered a "glaucoma suspect"

□ Summarize the clinical features, evaluation, and therapy of normal-tension glaucoma

□ List various clinical features of and therapeutic approaches for the primary and secondary open-angle glaucomas

□ Explain the impact of new technology on our understanding of various forms of secondary open-angle glaucoma

□ Review the mechanisms and pathophysiology of primary angle-closure glaucoma, both with and without pupillary block

□ Review the pathophysiology of secondary angle-closure glaucoma, both with and without pupillary block

□ Outline the pathophysiology and therapy of childhood glaucoma

□ Differentiate among the various classes of medical therapy for glaucoma

□ Compare the indications and techniques of various laser procedures and incisional filtering surgical procedures for glaucoma

□ Describe cyclodestructive treatment for refractory glaucoma

□ Summarize the indications for and use of low-vision aids in glaucoma patients

INTRODUCTION TO SECTION 10

Section 10 of the Basic and Clinical Science Course is devoted to glaucoma. The diseases associated with glaucoma that are discussed in this section are commonly encountered in ophthalmic practice; however, management of many of these conditions is controversial. We will discuss only the major prevailing approaches. Surgical management is continually changing with the development of new instruments and techniques. Only general surgical principles are emphasized in this Section. Specific details of surgical technique are better learned at a practice laboratory and in the operating room with an experienced teacher, as well as through textbooks, original articles, and courses designed specifically for this purpose.

Development of Our Concept of Glaucoma

The word *glaucoma* derives from the Greek word *glaukós,* which means a watery or diluted blue. Hippocrates mentioned the condition of glaukosis among the infirmities that old people suffer. Hippocrates meant by the term a bluish discoloration of the pupil. The condition was later called *ypochýma* and corresponded to a cataract.

In antiquity it was assumed that glaukosis and hypochyma were identical. Later, during the Alexandrian time, glaucoma was thought to be a disease of the crystalline body (or fluid), which changed its normal color to light blue; hypochyma, in contrast, was regarded as the exudation of a fluid that later congealed and lay between the iris and the lens. All glaucomas were considered incurable, while it was believed that some hypochymata could be improved.

During the Middle Ages, the School of Salerno introduced the concept of "gutta serena," which was supposed to be one type of incurable cataract in which the pupil was dilated and clear; the condition was considered to be possibly congenital. According to this School, another type of incurable cataract existed in which the pupil would dilate suddenly and appear green.

The authors of antiquity and the Arabian physicians interpreted glaucoma as an incurable cataract with desiccation of the lens. Pierre Brisseau, with his little book on cataract and glaucoma published in 1709, was the first to consider glaucoma as a vitreous opacification. He correctly interpreted the cataract as an opaque crystalline lens.

The first reasonably satisfactory description of glaucoma was written by Charles St. Yves (1722): "Glaucoma is one of the spurious cataracts. First the patients see smoke and fog; then they lose vision while the pupil becomes dilated; finally, only a remnant of vision remains temporally. The disease may begin with severe pain. The prognosis is poor. There is danger that the other eye will also be affected."

Johann Zacharias Platner (1745) was the first to state that the glaucomatous eye was hard, resisting the pressure exerted by the fingers. The pressure theory was then emphasized and clarified by William Mackenzie (1830). Jakob Wenzel (1808) thought that glaucoma was primarily a disease of the retina, while S. Canstatt (1831), Julius Sichel (1841), and followers declared glaucoma a form of choroiditis. All of them considered glaucoma incurable. Georg Josef Beer (1817) thought that glaucoma was an opacification of the vitreous and the sequel of an arthritic ophthalmia that would only develop in patients with gout who had had no preceding ocular inflammation.

A few futile attempts were made to treat glaucoma. Mackenzie suggested a sclerotomy or lensectomy. Georg Stromeyer recommended tenotomy of the superior oblique and myotomy of the inferior oblique. St. Yves wanted to enucleate the affected eye to prevent involvement of the second eye. The first real breakthrough in treatment was the discovery in 1856 by Albrecht von Graefe that iridectomy could be a curative procedure for certain types of glaucoma. He had first tried without success the instillation of atropine and repeated paracenteses to lower IOP.

Only with the invention of the ophthalmoscope was it possible to observe the changes in the optic nerve head associated with glaucoma. The term *pressure excavation* had been coined by von Graefe. This ophthalmoscopic concept was corroborated by careful pathologic examinations initiated by Heinrich Müller. Edward Jaeger and Isidor Schnabel defended the hypothesis that glaucoma was characterized by specific optic nerve disease.

It soon became obvious that an iridectomy could not cure all types of glaucoma. Albrecht von Graefe had already noted that a cystoid scar would offer certain advantages for normalizing IOP. Sclerotomy was first proposed by Louis de Wecker in 1869. Surgeons then tried to keep the wound open on purpose, either by infolding of the conjunctiva (H. Herbert, 1903) or by incarceration of the iris (George Critchett of London in 1858 and Soren Holth of Oslo in 1904). Finally, the iridosclerectomy was devised by Pierre Lagrange in Paris (1905), and the trephining operation introduced by Robert H. Elliot of Madras, India. Thermosclerotomy was first described by Luigi Preziosi of Malta in 1924. It was later modified and popularized by Harold Scheie of Philadelphia in 1958.

The medical treatment of glaucoma was initiated with eserine, which is derived from the Calabar bean of West Africa. This drug was first recognized as a miotic, and it was used for treating iris prolapse. In 1876 Ludwig Laqueur of Strasbourg and Adolf Weber of Darmstadt were the first to use eserine to treat glaucoma. The alkaloid pilocarpine was isolated in 1875. It was first topically applied to the eye by John Tweedy of London (1875) and by Weber (1876) in an effort to lower IOP.

Frederick C. Blodi, MD

CHAPTER 1

Introduction and Definitions

Glaucoma refers to a group of diseases that have in common a characteristic *optic neuropathy* with associated *visual field loss* for which *elevated intraocular pressure (IOP)* is one of the primary risk factors. There are several risk factors for the development of glaucoma, many of which remain unknown. Three factors determine the IOP (Fig 1-1):

☐ The rate of aqueous humor production by the ciliary body

☐ Resistance to aqueous outflow across the trabecular meshwork–Schlemm's canal system

☐ The level of episcleral venous pressure

The commonly accepted range for normal IOP in the general population is 10–21 mm Hg. In most cases increased IOP is caused by increased resistance to aqueous humor outflow.

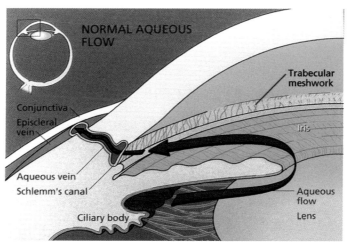

FIG 1-1—Diagrammatic cross section of the anterior segment of the normal eye, showing the site of aqueous production (ciliary body) and sites of resistance to aqueous outflow (trabecular meshwork–Schlemm's canal system and episcleral venous plexus).

In most individuals the optic nerve and visual field changes in glaucoma are determined by both the level of the IOP and the optic nerve axons' resistance to pressure damage. Other factors also seem to predispose the optic nerve axons to damage. Although progressive changes in the visual field and optic nerve are usually related to increased IOP, in cases of normal-tension, or low-tension, glaucoma the IOP remains within the normal range. In most cases of glaucoma the IOP is too high for proper functioning of the optic nerve axons, and lowering the IOP will stabilize the damage. In cases involving other pathophysiologic mechanisms that may affect the optic nerve, progression of optic nerve damage may continue despite lowering of IOP.

The *primary glaucomas,* by definition, are not associated with known ocular or systemic disorders that cause increased resistance to aqueous outflow. The primary glaucomas usually affect both eyes and may be inherited. Conversely, the *secondary glaucomas* are associated with ocular or systemic disorders responsible for decreased aqueous outflow. The diseases that cause secondary glaucoma are often unilateral, and familial occurrence is less common.

CHAPTER II

Social and Economic Aspects of Glaucoma

Glaucoma is an important cause of blindness in the United States and the most frequent cause of blindness in black Americans. Between 80,000 and 116,000 Americans are legally blind as a result of glaucoma, and it is estimated that each year an additional 5,500 people become legally blind in the United States. Legal blindness is defined as a visual acuity of 20/200 or poorer in the better eye with correction or a visual field no greater than 20° in its widest diameter. Almost 900,000 people in the United States are visually impaired (defined as having some chronic or permanent defect in vision) as a result of glaucoma. Approximately 2.25 million Americans 40 years or older have primary open-angle glaucoma, and other forms of glaucoma or related conditions add to these totals. Perhaps one half of these people are not aware of their disease. Elevated IOP is estimated to affect 5–10 million Americans, placing them at higher risk for developing glaucomatous optic nerve damage.

Estimates of worldwide blindness caused by primary open-angle glaucoma exceed 3 million cases. More than 100 million people throughout the world have elevated IOP, and approximately 2.4 million develop primary open-angle glaucoma each year.

In the United States more than 3 million office visits per year are made to monitor glaucoma, and more than 1 million patients are under treatment. According to projections from sample data, direct health care costs for glaucoma exceeded $400 million in 1977, and an estimated $1.3 billion was lost because of decreased productivity. More recent figures show more than $1 billion spent on federal assistance to blind glaucoma patients through disability, Medicare, and Medicaid payments and income tax credits. Even though these estimates are only approximate, it is clear that glaucoma is a very important public health problem.

National Advisory Eye Counsel. *Vision Research—A National Plan: 1982.* Washington, DC: National Institutes of Health; 1982;1:12–13.

Preferred Practice Patterns Committee, Glaucoma Panel. *Primary Open-Angle Glaucoma.* San Francisco: American Academy of Ophthalmology; 1996.

CHAPTER III

Hereditary and Genetic Factors

Many hereditary and genetic influences are known to be factors in primary open-angle glaucoma. Whereas the prevalence of glaucoma is 1.5%–2.0% in the general population, 10%–15% of first-degree relatives of individuals with primary open-angle glaucoma are likely to develop the disease. In addition, other factors including IOP, size of the optic disc cup, outflow facility, angle configuration, and steroid responsiveness are at least in part influenced by heredity.

Both autosomal recessive and autosomal dominant modes of inheritance of open-angle glaucoma have been described in the literature. Adult-onset primary open-angle glaucoma is most consistent with an autosomal recessive transmission, which is also perhaps polygenic (involving more than one gene) and multifactorial (environmental and other nongenetic factors may influence the phenotypic manifestations). Autosomal dominant inheritance is characteristic of juvenile-onset open-angle glaucoma.

Recently, large pedigree studies have linked the disease to chromosome 1q. In these families onset of severe glaucoma generally occurred in the second to third decade of life and was associated with high IOP that was refractory to medical therapy. Most cases required filtering surgery.

Future pedigree studies will undoubtably offer more clues to the nature of other forms of glaucoma. Once the genetic defects are identified, the individual protein anomalies that are encoded by these genes can be identified. This decoding may lead to specific therapeutic approaches for the various forms of glaucoma.

CHAPTER IV

Classification

A number of schemes for classifying glaucoma have been proposed. They are based on the age of the patient (infantile, juvenile, adult); the site of obstruction to aqueous outflow (pretrabecular, trabecular, posttrabecular); the tissue principally involved (e.g., glaucoma caused by diseases of the lens); and etiology (e.g., neovascular glaucoma resulting from central retinal vein occlusion). Another useful system differentiates glaucomatous conditions caused by internal obstruction of aqueous flow (e.g., pupillary block or ciliary block) from those caused by external obstruction of aqueous outflow (e.g., impaired direct outflow or increased episcleral venous pressure). Although each of these systems has value, a classification scheme that separates open-angle from angle-closure glaucoma has been most widely used, because it focuses on pathophysiology and creates a starting point for proper clinical management.

In open-angle glaucoma, outflow of aqueous humor through the trabecular meshwork–Schlemm's canal venous system is impaired (Fig IV-1). In angle-closure glaucoma, resistance to outflow is increased because the peripheral iris obstructs the trabecular meshwork (Fig IV-2). Table IV-1 lists the types of glaucoma with their characteristics.

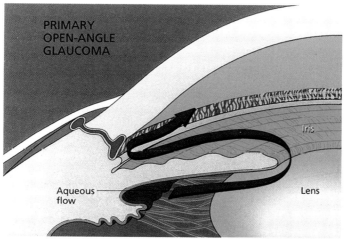

FIG IV-1—Schematic of open-angle glaucoma with resistance to aqueous outflow through the trabecular meshwork–Schlemm's canal system in the absence of gross anatomic obstruction.

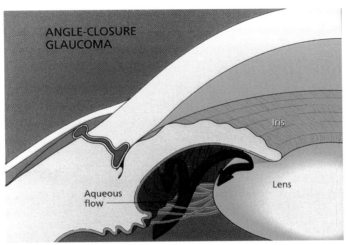

FIG IV-2—Schematic of angle-closure glaucoma with pupillary block leading to peripheral iris obstruction of the trabecular meshwork.

TABLE IV-1

CLASSIFICATION OF GLAUCOMA

TYPE	CHARACTERISTICS
Open-angle glaucoma	
Primary open-angle glaucoma	Optic nerve damage and visual field loss associated with elevated IOP
	Cause of trabecular obstruction not known
Glaucoma suspect	Normal optic disc and visual field associated with elevated IOP
	Suspicious optic disc and/or visual field with normal IOP
Normal-tension glaucoma	Optic nerve damage and visual field loss associated with normal IOP
Secondary open-angle glaucoma	Increased resistance to trabecular meshwork outflow associated with other conditions (e.g., pigmentary glaucoma, phacolytic glaucoma, steroid-induced glaucoma)
	Increased posttrabecular resistance to outflow secondary to elevated episcleral venous pressure (e.g., carotid cavernous sinus fistula)

TABLE IV-1

CLASSIFICATION OF GLAUCOMA (continued)

TYPE	CHARACTERISTICS
Angle-closure glaucoma	
Primary angle-closure glaucoma with relative pupillary block	Movement of aqueous humor from posterior chamber to anterior chamber restricted; peripheral iris in contact with trabecular meshwork
Primary angle-closure glaucoma without pupillary block	(E.g., plateau iris)
Secondary angle-closure glaucoma with pupillary block	(E.g., swollen lens, secluded pupil)
Secondary angle-closure glaucoma without pupillary block	Posterior pushing mechanism: lens–iris diaphragm pushed forward (e.g., posterior segment tumor, scleral buckling procedure, uveal effusion)
	Anterior pulling mechanism: anterior segment process pulling iris forward to form peripheral anterior synechiae (e.g., iridocorneal endothelial syndrome, neovascular glaucoma, inflammation)
Combined-mechanism glaucoma	
A combination of two or more forms of glaucoma	(E.g., open-angle glaucoma in a patient who develops secondary angle closure following a scleral buckling procedure)
Childhood glaucoma	
Primary congenital/ infantile glaucoma	
Glaucoma associated with congenital anomalies	Associated with ocular disorders (e.g., anterior segment dysgenesis, aniridia)
	Associated with systemic disorders (e.g., rubella, Lowe syndrome)
Secondary glaucoma in infants and children	(E.g., glaucoma secondary to retinoblastoma or trauma)

CHAPTER V

Intraocular Pressure and Aqueous Humor Dynamics

The ciliary processes produce *aqueous humor,* which flows from the posterior chamber through the pupil into the anterior chamber. Aqueous humor exits the eye by passing through the *trabecular meshwork* into *Schlemm's canal* and then draining into the venous system through a plexus of collector channels. The Goldmann equation summarizes the relationship between these factors and the IOP in the undisturbed eye:

$$P_0 = (F/C) + P_v$$

in which P_0 is the IOP in millimeters of mercury (mm Hg), F is the rate of aqueous formation in microliters per minute (μl/min), C is the facility of outflow in microliters per minute per millimeter of mercury (μl/min/mm Hg), and P_v is the episcleral venous pressure in millimeters of mercury. Resistance to outflow (R) is the inverse of facility (C) and may replace C in rearrangements of the Goldmann equation.

Aqueous Humor Formation

Aqueous humor is formed by the *ciliary processes,* each of which is composed of a double layer of epithelium over a core of stroma and a rich supply of fenestrated capillaries. The apical layers of the outer pigmented layer of epithelium and the inner nonpigmented layer face each other and are joined by tight junctions, which are probably an important part of the blood-aqueous barrier. The nonpigmented epithelial cells contain numerous mitochondria and microvilli and are thought to be the site of aqueous production (Fig V-1). The ciliary processes provide a large surface area for secretion. A detailed description of the aqueous humor composition is found in BCSC Section 2, *Fundamentals and Principles of Ophthalmology.*

Aqueous humor formation is not precisely understood, but it involves the combination of active transport (secretion), ultrafiltration, and simple diffusion. *Active transport* consumes energy to move substances against an electrochemical gradient and is independent of pressure. The identity of the precise ion or ions transported is not known, but sodium, chloride, and bicarbonate are involved. The majority of aqueous production results from active transport. *Ultrafiltration* refers to a pressure-dependent movement along a pressure gradient. In the ciliary processes the hydrostatic pressure difference between capillary pressure and IOP favors fluid movement into the eye, while the oncotic gradient between the two resists fluid movement. The relationship between secretion and ultrafiltration is not known.

The mechanisms of action of the two classes of drugs that suppress aqueous formation, *carbonic anhydrase inhibitors* and *beta-adrenergic antagonists,* are also not precisely understood. The role of the enzyme carbonic anhydrase has been debated

Posterior Chamber

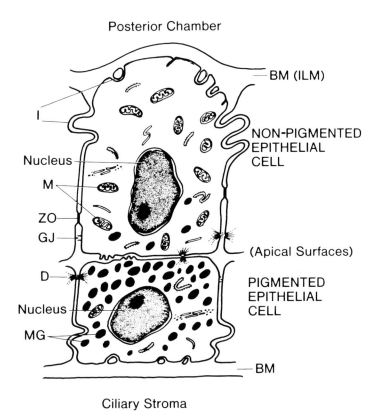

FIG V-1—The two layers of the ciliary epithelium. Apical surfaces are in apposition to each other. Basement membrane (*BM*) lines the double layer and constitutes the internal limiting membrane (*ILM*) on the inner surface. The nonpigmented epithelium is characterized by mitochondria (*M*), zonula occludens (*ZO*), and lateral and surface interdigitations (*I*). The pigmented epithelium contains numerous melanin granules (*MG*). Additional intercellular junctions include desmosomes (*D*) and gap junctions (*GJ*). (Reproduced with permission from Shields MB. *Textbook of Glaucoma*. 3rd ed. Baltimore: Williams & Wilkins; 1992.)

vigorously. Evidence suggests that the bicarbonate ion is actively secreted in human eyes; thus, the function of the enzyme may be to provide this ion. Carbonic anhydrase may also provide bicarbonate or hydrogen ions for an intracellular buffering system.

Current evidence indicates that beta$_2$ receptors are the most prevalent adrenergic receptors in the ciliary epithelium. The significance of this finding is unclear, but beta-adrenergic antagonists may affect active transport by causing a decrease in the efficiency of the Na^+/K^+ pump or a decrease in the number of pump sites. (For a detailed discussion of the sodium pump and pump/leak mechanism, see BCSC Section 2, *Fundamentals and Principles of Ophthalmology,* and BCSC Section 11, *Lens and Cataract.*)

The most common method used to measure the rate of aqueous formation is *fluorophotometry.* Fluorescein is administered systemically or topically, and the subsequent decline in its anterior chamber concentration is measured optically and used to calculate aqueous flow. Normal flow is approximately 2–3 μl/min, or a 1% turnover in aqueous volume per minute.

Aqueous formation varies diurnally and drops during sleep. It also decreases with age, as does outflow facility. The rate of aqueous formation is affected by a variety of factors, including the integrity of the blood-aqueous barrier, blood flow to the ciliary body, and neurohumoral regulation of vascular tissue and the ciliary epithelium. Aqueous inflow falls when the eye is injured or inflamed and following the administration of certain drugs such as general anesthetics and some systemic hypotensive agents. Carotid occlusive disease may also decrease aqueous humor production.

Aqueous Humor Outflow

The facility of outflow (C in the Goldmann equation; see page 14) varies widely in normal eyes. The mean value reported ranges from 0.22 to 0.28 μl/min/mm Hg. Outflow facility decreases with age and is affected by surgery, trauma, medications, and endocrine factors. Patients with glaucoma usually have decreased outflow facility.

Trabecular Outflow

Most of the aqueous humor exits the eye through the trabecular meshwork/ Schlemm's canal/venous system. The trabecular meshwork can be divided into three zones: uveal, corneoscleral, and juxtacanalicular (Fig V-2). The primary resistance to outflow occurs at the juxtacanalicular tissue. The trabecular meshwork functions as a one-way valve that permits aqueous to leave the eye by bulk flow but limits flow in the other direction independently of energy. Aqueous moves both across and between the endothelial cells lining the inner wall of Schlemm's canal. Once in Schlemm's canal, aqueous enters the episcleral venous plexus by way of scleral collector channels. When IOP is low, the trabecular meshwork collapses, which reduces backflow and prevents most proteins and blood cells from reaching the optical media.

Uveoscleral Outflow

In the normal eye any nontrabecular outflow is termed uveoscleral outflow. A variety of mechanisms are involved, predominantly aqueous passage from the anterior chamber into the ciliary muscle and then into the supraciliary and suprachoroidal spaces. The fluid then exits the eye through the intact sclera or along the nerves and vessels that penetrate it. Uveoscleral outflow, which may account for as much as 20% of aqueous outflow in normal eyes, is pressure-dependent. It is increased by cycloplegic agents, epinephrine, apraclonidine, and certain forms of surgery (e.g., cyclodialysis) and is decreased by miotics.

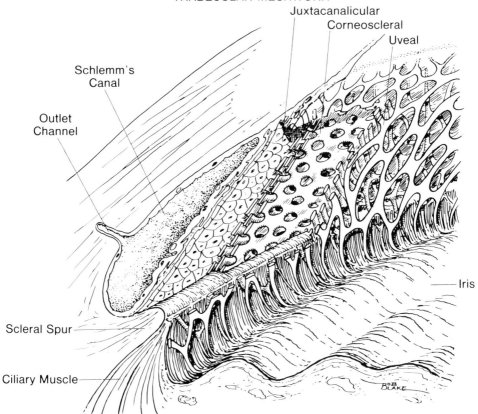

TRABECULAR MESHWORK

Juxtacanalicular

Corneoscleral

Uveal

Schlemm's
Canal

Outlet
Channel

Iris

Scleral Spur

Ciliary Muscle

FIG V-2—Three layers of trabecular meshwork (shown in cutaway views): uveal, corneoscleral, and juxtacanalicular. (Reproduced with permission from Shields MB. *Textbook of Glaucoma.* 3rd ed. Baltimore: Williams & Wilkins; 1992.)

Tonography

The ease with which aqueous can leave the eye is measured by tonography as the facility of outflow. This measurement is taken using a Schiøtz tonometer of known weight, which is placed on the cornea, suddenly elevating IOP. The rate at which the pressure declines with time is related to the ease with which the aqueous leaves the eye. The decline in IOP over time can be used to determine outflow facility in µl/min/mm Hg through a series of mathematical calculations.

Unfortunately, tonography depends upon a number of assumptions (e.g., the elastic properties of the eye, stability of aqueous formation, constancy of ocular blood volume) and is subject to many sources of error (e.g., calibration problems, patient fixation, eyelid squeezing, technician errors). These problems reduce the accuracy and reproducibility of tonography for an individual patient. At present, tonography is best used as a research tool for the investigation of matters such as drug effects. It is rarely used clinically.

Episcleral Venous Pressure

Episcleral venous pressure is relatively stable, except when alterations in body position and certain diseases of the orbit, head, and neck obstruct venous return to the heart or shunt blood from the arterial to the venous system. The usual range of values is 8–12 mm Hg. The pressure in the episcleral veins can be measured with specialized equipment. In acute conditions, IOP rises approximately 1 mm Hg for every 1 mm Hg increase in episcleral venous pressure. The relationship is more complex, however, in chronic conditions. Chronic elevations of episcleral venous pressure may be accompanied by changes in IOP that are of greater, lesser, or the same magnitude.

Intraocular Pressure

Distribution in the Population and Relation to Glaucoma

Pooled data from large epidemiological studies indicate that the mean IOP is approximately 16 mm Hg, with a standard deviation of 3 mm Hg. The pressure has a non-gaussian distribution with a skew toward higher pressures, especially in individuals over 40 (Fig V-3). In the past, the value 21 mm Hg was used both to separate normal and abnormal pressures and to define which patients required ocular hypotensive therapy. This division was based largely on the erroneous assumptions that glaucomatous damage is caused exclusively by pressures that are higher than normal and that normal pressures do not cause damage.

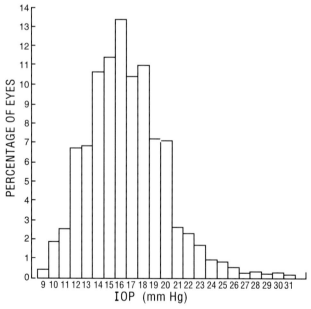

FIG V-3—Frequency distribution of intraocular pressure: 5220 eyes in the Framingham Eye Study. (Reproduced from Colton T, Ederer F. The distribution of intraocular pressures in the general population. *Surv Ophthalmol.* 1980;25:123–129.)

There is general agreement now that, for the population as a whole, no clear line exists between safe and unsafe IOP; some eyes undergo damage at IOPs of 18 mm Hg or less, while others tolerate IOPs in the 30s. However, IOP is still seen as a very important risk factor for the development of glaucomatous damage. Although other risk factors affect an individual's susceptibility to glaucomatous damage, IOP is the only one that can be altered at this time.

Factors Influencing Intraocular Pressure

IOP varies with a number of factors, including

- Time of day
- Season
- Heartbeat
- Respiration
- Exercise
- Fluid intake
- Systemic medications
- Topical drugs

Alcohol consumption results in a transient decrease in IOP. Caffeine may cause a small, transient rise in IOP. Cannabis decreases IOP, but its clinical utility is not established. IOP is higher when the patient is recumbent rather than upright. Some people have an exaggerated rise in IOP when they lie down, and this tendency may be important in the pathogenesis of some forms of glaucoma. IOP usually increases with age and is genetically influenced: higher pressures are more common in relatives of patients with primary open-angle glaucoma than in the general population.

Diurnal Variation

In normal individuals IOP varies 2–6 mm Hg over a 24-hour period as aqueous humor production changes. The higher the pressure, the greater the fluctuation, and a diurnal fluctuation of greater than 10 mm Hg is suggestive of glaucoma. Many people reach their peak pressures in the morning hours, but others do so in the afternoon or evening, and still others follow no reproducible pattern. To detect such fluctuations, ocular pressure is measured at multiple times around the clock. These measurements can sometimes be useful in evaluating suspected normal-tension glaucoma, assessing the effect that therapy changes have on pressure control, and determining why optic nerve damage might occur despite apparently good control of pressure.

Clinical Measurement of Intraocular Pressure

Measurement of IOP in a clinical setting requires a force that indents or flattens the eye. The two methods used widely are *applanation tonometry* and *Schiøtz (indentation) tonometry*. Applanation tonometry is based on the Imbert-Fick principle, which states that the pressure inside an ideal dry, thin-walled sphere equals the force necessary to flatten its surface divided by the area of the flattening.

$$P = F/A \text{ (where } P = \text{pressure, } F = \text{force, } A = \text{area)}$$

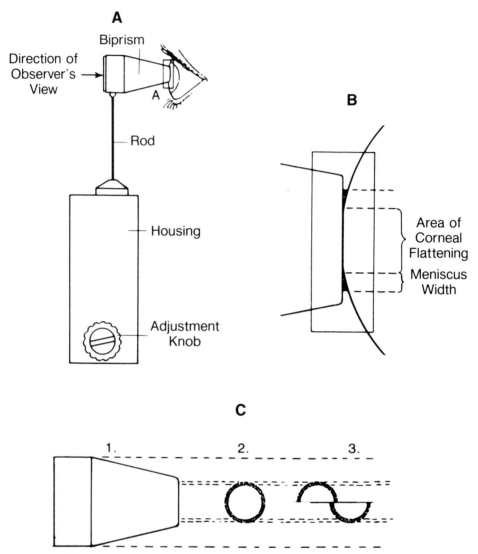

A

Biprism

Direction of
Observer's
View

A

Rod

Housing

Adjustment
Knob

B

Area of
Corneal
Flattening

Meniscus
Width

C

1.

2.

3.

FIG V-4—Goldmann-type applanation tonometry. *A,* Basic features of tonometer, shown in contact with patient's cornea. *B,* Enlargement shows tear-film meniscus created by contact of biprism and cornea. *C,* View through biprism *(1)* reveals circular meniscus *(2),* which is converted into semicircle *(3)* by prisms. (Reproduced with permission from Shields MB. *Textbook of Glaucoma.* 3rd ed. Baltimore: Williams & Wilkins; 1992.)

In applanation tonometry the cornea is flattened, and IOP is determined by measuring the applanating force and the area flattened (Fig V-4).

The Goldmann applanation tonometer measures the force necessary to flatten an area of the cornea of 3.06 mm diameter. At this diameter the resistance of the

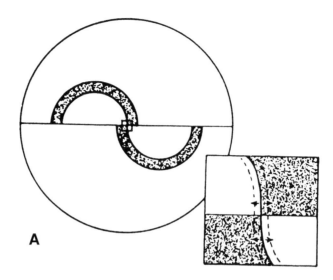

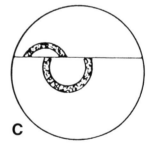

A

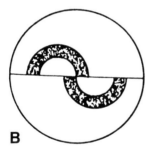

B   C

FIG V-5—Semicircles of Goldmann-type applanation tonometer. *A*, Proper width and position. Enlargement depicts excursions of semicircles caused by ocular pulsations. *B*, Semicircles are too wide. *C*, Improper vertical and horizontal alignment. (Reproduced with permission from Shields MB. *Textbook of Glaucoma.* 3rd ed. Baltimore: Williams & Wilkins; 1992.)

cornea to flattening is counterbalanced by the capillary attraction of the tear meniscus for the tonometer head. Furthermore, the IOP (in mm Hg) equals the flattening force (in grams) multiplied by 10. A split-image device allows the examiner to determine the flattened area with great accuracy. Fluorescein in the tear film is used to outline the area of flattening. The semicircles move with the ocular pulse, and the end point is reached when the inner edges of the semicircles touch each other at the midpoint of their excursion (Fig V-5).

Applanation measurements are safe, easy to perform, and relatively accurate in most clinical situations. Of the currently available devices, the Goldmann applanation tonometer is the most valid and reliable. Since applanation does not displace much fluid (approximately 0.5 µl) or substantially increase the pressure in the eye, this method is relatively unaffected by ocular rigidity.

Possible sources of error include squeezing of the eyelids, breath holding or Valsalva's maneuvers, pressure on the globe, extraocular muscle force applied to a restricted globe, tight collars, and an inaccurately calibrated tonometer. Excessive fluorescein results in wide mires and an inaccurately high reading, whereas inadequate fluorescein leads to low readings. Marked corneal astigmatism causes an elliptical fluorescein pattern. To obtain an accurate reading, the clinician should rotate the prism so that the red mark on the prism holder is set at the least curved meridian of the cornea (along the negative axis). Alternately, two pressure readings taken 90° apart can be averaged.

The accuracy of applanation tonometry is reduced in certain situations. Corneal edema predisposes to inaccurately low readings, whereas pressure measurements taken over a corneal scar will be falsely high. Tonometry performed over a soft contact lens gives falsely low values. Alterations in scleral rigidity may compromise the accuracy of measurements; for example, applanation readings that follow scleral buckling procedures may be inaccurately low.

The *Perkins tonometer* is a counterbalanced tonometer that is portable and can be used with the patient either upright or supine. It is similar to the Goldmann tonometer in using a split-image device and fluorescein staining of the tears.

Noncontact (air-puff) tonometers measure IOP without touching the eye, by measuring the time necessary for a given force of air to flatten a given area of the cornea. Readings obtained with these instruments vary widely, and they often overestimate IOP. These instruments are often used in large-scale glaucoma-screening programs.

The group of *portable electronic applanation devices* (e.g., Tonopen) that applanate a very small area of the cornea are particularly useful in the presence of corneal scars or edema. The *pneumatic tonometer* has a pressure-sensing device that consists of a gas-filled chamber covered by a Silastic diaphragm. The gas in the chamber escapes through an exhaust vent. As the diaphragm touches the cornea, the gas vent is reduced in size and the pressure in the chamber rises. Because this instrument, too, applanates only a small area of the cornea, it is especially useful in the presence of corneal scars or edema.

Schiøtz tonometry determines IOP by measuring the indentation of the cornea produced by a known weight (Fig V-6). The indentation is read on a linear scale on the instrument and is converted to mm Hg by a calibration table. The indentation technique attempts to estimate IOP before the weight is placed on the eye. This estimate depends on a number of factors, including standard corneal curvature and elastic properties of the eye. Indentation tonometry gives falsely low readings when scleral rigidity is reduced (i.e., in the presence of high myopia, treatment with cholinesterase inhibitors, thyroid disease, and previous ocular surgery including cataract extraction). The accuracy of indentation tonometry may also be reduced by incorrect technique, inadequate cleaning (the instrument is difficult to clean both quickly and adequately), and improper calibration. This tonometer has the advan-

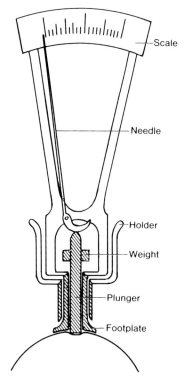

FIG V-6—Cutaway view showing basic features of Schiøtz-type indentation tonometer. (Reproduced with permission from Shields MB. *Textbook of Glaucoma.* 3rd ed. Baltimore: Williams & Wilkins; 1992.)

tage of simple construction, portability, ease of use, and low cost. Because of a number of practical and theoretical problems, however, Schiøtz tonometry is now used much less frequently than in past years. The application of a relatively heavy weight to the eye causes a large rise in IOP. The Schiøtz tonometer is most useful in family physicians' offices and for home tonometry.

It is possible to estimate IOP by *digital pressure* on the globe. This test may be used with uncooperative patients, but it may be inaccurate even in very experienced hands. In general, tactile tensions are only useful for detecting large differences between two eyes.

Infection Control in Clinical Tonometry

Many infectious agents, including the viruses responsible for AIDS, hepatitis, and epidemic keratoconjunctivitis, can be recovered from tears. To prevent transfer of such agents, tonometers must be cleaned after each use.

☐ The prism head of both the Goldmann-type tonometer and the Perkins tonometer should be cleaned immediately after use. The prisms should either be soaked in a 1:10 sodium hypochlorite solution or be thoroughly wiped with 70% ethanol. If a soaking solution is used, the prism should be rinsed and dried before reuse. If alcohol is employed, it should be allowed to evaporate, or the prism head should be dried before reuse, to prevent damage to the epithelium.

☐ The air-puff tonometer front surface should be wiped with alcohol between uses because tears from the patient may contaminate the instrument.

☐ The portable electronic applanation devices employ a disposable cover, which should be replaced immediately after each use.

☐ The Schiøtz tonometer requires disassembly to clean both the plunger and the footplate. Unless the plunger is clean (as opposed to sterile), the measurements may be falsely elevated because of increased friction between the plunger and the footplate. The inside of the footplate can be cleaned of tears and any tear-film debris with a pipe cleaner. The same solutions used for cleaning prism heads may then be employed to sterilize the instrument.

For other tonometers, consult the manufacturer's recommendations.

CHAPTER VI

Clinical Evaluation

History and General Examination

Appropriate management of glaucoma depends on the clinician's ability to diagnose the specific form of glaucoma in a given patient and to determine the severity of the condition. The aspects of a clinical evaluation most important in assessment of a glaucoma patient are discussed below.

History

The history should include the following:

- The patient's current complaint
- Ocular history
- General medical history
- Family history of glaucoma and other ocular disease

It is often useful to question the patient specifically regarding symptoms and conditions sometimes related to glaucoma, such as pain, redness, halo vision, blurring of vision, trauma, surgery, and prior ocular diseases. Similarly, the general medical history should include specific inquiry regarding diseases that may have ocular manifestations or may affect the patient's ability to tolerate medication. Such conditions include diabetes, cardiac and pulmonary disease, hypertension, shock, migraine and other neurological diseases, and renal stones. In addition to identifying present medications and medication allergies, the clinician should take note of a history of corticosteroid use.

Refraction

Neutralizing any refractive error is crucial for accurate perimetry. Highly hyperopic eyes are at increased risk of angle-closure glaucoma; whether myopic eyes have increased risk of open-angle glaucoma remains controversial.

Pupils

Pupil size may be affected by glaucoma therapy. In patients who are on miotic therapy, pupillary responses are one measure of compliance. Testing for an afferent pupillary defect may detect asymmetric optic nerve damage.

Biomicroscopy

Biomicroscopy of the anterior segment is performed for signs of underlying or associated ocular disease.

Conjunctiva   Eyes with acutely elevated IOP may have conjunctival vasodilation. Chronic use of sympathomimetic drops may also cause conjunctival infection, and chronic use of epinephrine derivatives may result in black adrenochrome deposits in the conjunctiva. The use of topical antiglaucoma medication can also cause decreased tear production, allergic reactions, and scarring.

Episclera and sclera   Dilation of the episcleral vessels may indicate elevated episcleral venous pressure, which occurs in Sturge-Weber syndrome or in arteriovenous fistulas.

Cornea   Enlargement of the cornea associated with breaks in Descemet's membrane is commonly found in infantile glaucoma patients. Glaucomas associated with other anterior segment anomalies are described subsequently. The presence of a Krukenberg spindle, anterior Schwalbe's line, corneal edema, endothelial abnormality, and traumatic or surgical corneal scars should be noted.

Anterior chamber   The depth of the chamber is discussed under Gonioscopy. The presence of inflammation should be determined prior to installation of eyedrops.

Iris   Examination should be performed prior to dilation. Heterochromia, iris atrophy, transillumination defects, ectropion uveae, corectopia, nevi, nodules, and exfoliative material should be noted. Early stages of neovascularization of the anterior segment appear as either fine nubbins around the pupil or as a fine network of vessels on the surface of the iris. The iris should also be examined for evidence of trauma, such as sphincter rupture or iridodonesis, and the presence of vitreous humor in the anterior chamber should be noted.

Lens   The lens is generally best examined after dilation. Exfoliative material, phacodonesis, and lens size, shape, and clarity should be noted. The presence, type, and position of an intraocular lens should be recorded along with the status of the posterior capsule.

Fundus   Fundus examination may reveal other, nonglaucomatous conditions. It should be performed with a dilated pupil.

Other Tests

Several tests may be helpful in selected patients, including fluorescein angiography, measurement of episcleral venous pressure, ophthalmodynamometry, ocular blood-flow measurements, ultrasonography, and optic nerve and nerve fiber layer photography. Although currently available in only a few centers, ultrasound biomicroscopy (UBM) provides valuable information about several types of glaucoma. The test employs shorter wavelength sound waves than does conventional ocular ultrasound, limiting the penetration but increasing the resolution tenfold. The test allows detailed examination of the anterior segment, the posterior chamber, and the ciliary body (Fig VI-1).

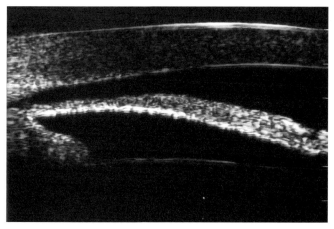

FIG VI-1—Pupillary block as shown by ultrasound biomicroscopy. Note the elevation above the lens of the peripheral iris on the left compared to the central iris on the right. (Photo courtesy of Charles J. Pavlin, MD.)

Gonioscopy

Gonioscopy is crucial for the proper diagnosis of glaucoma. Furthermore, gonioscopic expertise is essential for accurate glaucoma treatment in the angle (e.g., laser trabeculoplasty). Gonioscopy should be performed on all patients able to cooperate with the test.

Under normal conditions the anterior chamber angle cannot be viewed directly through the cornea, because light coming from the angle undergoes total internal reflection at the cornea-air interface. Gonioscopy eliminates this interface (the index of refraction of glass or plastic being similar to that of the cornea and tears) and replaces it with a new lens-air interface set at a different angle to the emerging rays. Depending on the type of lens employed, the angle can be examined with a direct system (Koeppe) or a mirrored indirect system (Goldmann or Zeiss) (Fig VI-2).

Direct gonioscopy is performed with a Koeppe lens, a binocular microscope, and a fiberoptic illuminator or slit-pen light. The Koeppe lens has a space that is filled with a saline solution or gonioscopic gel to couple it optically to the cornea. This system requires the patient to be supine. The Koeppe lens provides a direct panoramic view of the angle. The examiner is able to vary the direction of the light and the direction of viewing, which is an aid in identifying landmarks and examining narrow angles. Koeppe gonioscopy is particularly useful for comparing angles or portions of angles; for example, to diagnose angle recession. The Koeppe lens and other direct lenses may be used in the operating room for examinations and for surgical procedures of the angle such as goniotomy. The smooth-domed variety of direct lens provides a good view of the fundus with a direct ophthalmoscope and high plus lens even through a very small pupil. It is especially helpful in individuals with nystagmus or irregular corneas. The major disadvantage of the Koeppe system is its inconvenience.

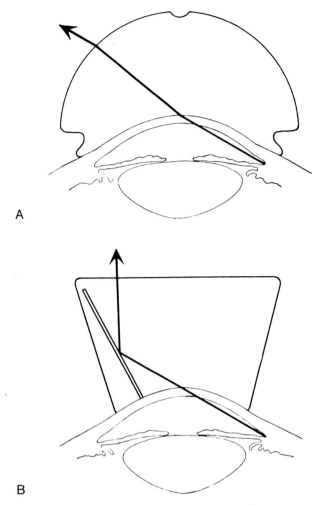

A

B

FIG VI-2—*A*, Direct gonioscopy. Diagram of rays of light from the angle emerging through a Koeppe lens. *B*, Indirect gonioscopy. Diagram of rays of light emerging through a Goldmann lens. (Reproduced with permission from Kolker AE, Hetherington J, eds. *Becker-Shaffer's Diagnosis and Therapy of the Glaucomas.* 5th ed. St Louis: CV Mosby Co; 1983.)

In contrast, once a patient is seated at the slit lamp for applanation tonometry, *indirect gonioscopy* can be performed rapidly and easily. Indirect gonioscopy employs a *goniolens* containing a mirror or mirrors. This instrument yields an inverted and slightly foreshortened image of the opposite angle. Although the image is inverted with an indirect goniolens, the right-left orientation of a horizontal mirror and the up-down orientation of a vertical mirror remain unchanged. The foreshortening, combined with the upright position of the patient, makes the angle appear a little shallower than it does with a Koeppe lens. Indirect goniolenses are used in conjunction with standard slit lamps, which provide magnification and illumination. Indirect goniolenses may also be used in the operating room in conjunction with a surgical microscope.

It may be difficult to examine the deepest aspect of a narrow angle with an indirect goniolens. Visibility can be improved by tilting the mirror toward the angle in question or rotating the eye toward the mirror, using a fixation light before the fellow eye.

The Goldmann goniolens requires a viscous fluid such as methylcellulose for optical coupling with the cornea. In lenses with only one mirror, the lens must be rotated to view the entire angle. Posterior pressure on the lens, especially if it is tilted, indents the sclera and falsely narrows the angle. The combination of lens manipulation and the use of viscous coupling fluid often temporarily reduces the clarity of the cornea and may make subsequent fundus examination and visual field testing more difficult.

The Zeiss lens and similar goniolenses with a smaller area of contact than the Goldmann lens have about the same radius of curvature as the cornea and are optically coupled by the patient's tears. Since the Zeiss-type lens has four mirrors, the entire angle is visible without rotation. The diameter of the lens is smaller than the diameter of the cornea, and pressure on the globe may distort the chamber angle. The examiner can detect this pressure by noting the induced folds in Descemet's membrane. Although pressure may falsely open the angle, indentation or compression (indentation gonioscopy) is useful in distinguishing iridocorneal apposition from synechial closure. Because of the small diameter of the Zeiss-type lens, pressure pushes aqueous humor from the center of the anterior chamber into the periphery. This action displaces iris tissue that is touching the trabecular meshwork, but it cannot displace peripheral anterior synechiae (Fig VI-3).

In performing both direct and indirect gonioscopy, the clinician must recognize the angle landmarks. The scleral spur and Schwalbe's line are the most important. With slit-lamp gonioscopy the examiner can locate Schwalbe's line at the termination of the corneal light wedge. Using a narrow slit beam and sharp focus, the examiner sees two linear reflections, one from the external surface of the cornea and its junction with the sclera, the other from the internal surface of the cornea. The two reflections meet at Schwalbe's line (Fig VI-4). The scleral spur is a thin, pale stripe between the ciliary face and the pigmented zone of the trabecular meshwork. The inferior portion of the angle is generally wider and is the easiest place in which to locate the landmarks. After verifying the landmarks, the clinician should examine the angle in an orderly manner (Table VI-1).

Proper management of glaucoma requires that the clinician determine whether the angle is open or closed. In angle closure, the peripheral iris obstructs the trabecular meshwork; i.e., the meshwork is not visible on gonioscopy. The width of the angle is determined by the site of insertion of the iris on the ciliary face, the convexity of the iris, and the prominence of the peripheral iris roll. In many cases the

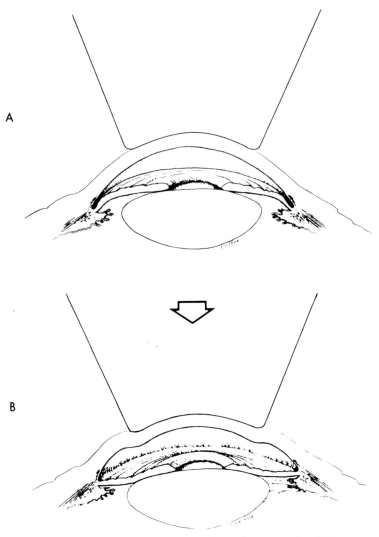

FIG VI-3—Pressure gonioscopy. Demonstration of the manner in which pressure on the cornea displaces iris to widen a narrow or closed anterior chamber angle. This maneuver exposes additional anatomical landmarks and is useful in determining the presence or absence of peripheral anterior synechiae. Synechiae, if present, can sometimes be separated. A, without pressure. B, with pressure. (Reproduced with permission from Hoskins HD Jr, Kass MA, eds. *Becker-Shaffer's Diagnosis and Therapy of the Glaucomas.* 6th ed. St Louis: CV Mosby Co; 1989.)

angle appears open but very narrow. It is often difficult to distinguish a narrow but open angle from an angle with partial closure; compression gonioscopy is useful in this situation (Fig VI-5).

To estimate the width of the chamber angle, the examiner directs a narrow slit beam at an angle of 60° onto the cornea just anterior to the limbus (Van Herick

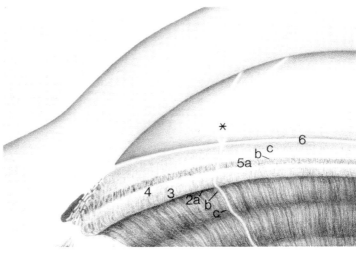

FIG VI-4—Gonioscopic appearance of a normal anterior chamber angle. *2,* Peripheral iris: *a,* insertion; *b,* curvature; *c,* angular approach. *3,* Ciliary body band. *4,* Scleral spur. *5,* Trabecular meshwork: *a,* posterior; *b,* mid; *c,* anterior. *6,* Schwalbe's line. *Asterisk,* Corneal optical wedge.

TABLE VI-1

GONIOSCOPIC EXAMINATION

TISSUE	FEATURES
Posterior cornea	Pigmentation
Schwalbe's line	Thickening, anterior displacement
Trabecular meshwork	Pigmentation, peripheral anterior synechiae, inflammatory or neovascular membranes, exudate
Scleral spur	Iris processes, presence or absence
Ciliary body band	Width, regularity, cyclodialysis cleft
Iris	Contour, rubeosis, atrophy, cysts, iridodonesis
Pupil and lens	Exfoliation syndrome, posterior synechiae, position and regularity, sphincter rupture, ectropion uveae
Zonular fibers	Pigmentation, rupture

method). If the distance from the anterior iris surface to the posterior surface of the cornea is less than one fourth the thickness of the cornea, the angle is narrow. This test should alert the examiner to narrow angles, but it is not a substitute for gonioscopy.

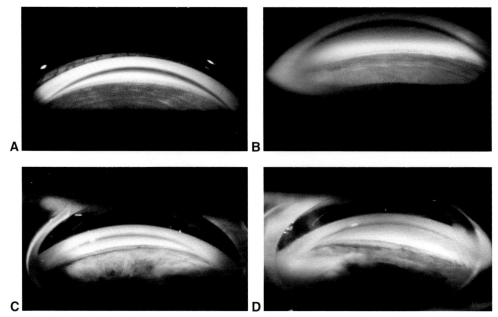

FIG VI-5—*A,* Normal open angle. Gonioscopic photograph shows trace pigmentation of the posterior trabecular meshwork and normal insertion of the iris into a narrow ciliary body band. The Goldmann lens was used. *B,* Normal open angle. This gonioscopic view using the Goldmann lens shows mild pigmentation of the posterior trabecular meshwork. A wide ciliary body band with posterior insertion of the iris can also be seen. *C,* Narrow angle. This gonioscopic view using the Zeiss lens without indentation shows pigment in inferior angle but poor visualization of angle anatomy. *D,* Narrow angle. Gonioscopy with a Zeiss lens with indentation shows peripheral anterior synechiae in the posterior trabecular meshwork. Pigment deposits on Schwalbe's line can also be seen. This is the same angle as shown in *C.*

The best method for describing the angle is a verbal description or drawing of the iris contour, the location of the iris insertion, and the angle between the iris and the trabecular meshwork. A variety of gonioscopic grading systems have been developed; the most commonly used are the Shaffer, Spaeth, and Scheie systems. Any grading system may eliminate some details, and a clinician who uses a grading system must specify which system is being used. The Shaffer system describes the angle between the trabecular meshwork and the iris as follows:

- *Grade IV.* The angle between the iris and the surface of the trabecular meshwork is 45°.

- *Grade III.* The angle between the iris and the surface of the trabecular meshwork is greater than 20° but less than 45°.

- *Grade II.* The angle between the iris and the surface of the trabecular meshwork is 20°. Angle closure possible.

- *Grade I.* The angle between the iris and the surface of the trabecular meshwork is 10°. Angle closure probable in time.
- *Slit.* The angle between the iris and the surface of the trabecular meshwork is less than 10°. Angle closure very likely.
- *0.* The iris is against the trabecular meshwork. Angle closure is present.

The Spaeth gonioscopic grading system expands this system to include a description of the peripheral iris contour and the effects of indentation gonioscopy on the angle configuration (Fig VI-6).

Ordinarily, Schlemm's canal is invisible by gonioscopy. Occasionally during gonioscopy in normal eyes, blood refluxes into Schlemm's canal where it is seen as a faint red line in the posterior portion of the trabecular meshwork. Blood enters Schlemm's canal when episcleral venous pressure exceeds IOP. The most common cause of this condition is compression of the episcleral veins by the lip of the goniolens. Pathological causes include hypotony and elevated episcleral venous pressure, as in carotid cavernous fistula or Sturge-Weber syndrome.

Normal blood vessels in the angle include radial iris vessels, portions of the arterial circle of the ciliary body, and vertical branches of the anterior ciliary arteries. Normal vessels are oriented either radially along the iris or circumferentially (in a serpentine manner) in the ciliary body face. Vessels that cross the scleral spur to reach the trabecular meshwork are usually abnormal (Fig VI-7). The vessels seen in Fuchs heterochromic iridocyclitis are fine, branching, unsheathed, and meandering. In patients who have neovascular glaucoma trunklike vessels cross the ciliary body and scleral spur and arborize over the trabecular meshwork. Contraction of the myofibroblasts accompanying these vessels leads to peripheral anterior synechiae (PAS) formation.

It is important to distinguish peripheral anterior synechiae from iris processes (uveal meshwork). Iris processes are open and lacy and follow the normal curve of the angle. The angle structures are visible in the open spaces between the processes. Synechiae are more solid or sheetlike (Fig VI-8). They are composed of iris stroma and obliterate the angle recess.

Pigmentation of the trabecular meshwork increases with age and is more marked in individuals with darkly pigmented irides. Pigmentation is usually most marked in the inferior angle. Heavy pigmentation of the trabecular meshwork should suggest pigment-dispersion syndrome or exfoliation syndrome. Other conditions that cause increased anterior chamber angle pigmentation include malignant melanoma, trauma, surgery, inflammation, and hyphema. Some of these conditions are associated with pigmentation anterior to Schwalbe's line.

Posttraumatic angle recession may be associated with monocular open-angle glaucoma. The gonioscopic criteria for diagnosing angle recession include an abnormally wide ciliary body band, increased prominence of the scleral spur, torn iris processes, sclera visible through disrupted ciliary body tissue, and marked variation of ciliary face width and angle depth in different quadrants of the same eye. In evaluating for angle recession, it is helpful to compare one portion of the angle to other areas in the same eye or to the same area in the fellow eye. This comparison is facilitated by performing simultaneous bilateral gonioscopy, which is easier with a Koeppe lens than with an indirect goniolens.

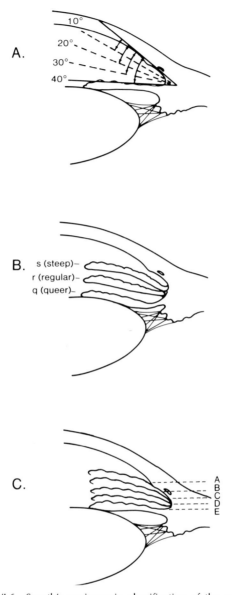

FIG VI-6—Spaeth's gonioscopic classification of the anterior chamber angle, based on three variables: *A,* angular width of the angle recess; *B,* configuration of the peripheral iris; and *C,* apparent insertion of the iris root. (Reproduced with permission from Shields MB. *Textbook of Glaucoma.* 3rd ed. Baltimore: Williams & Wilkins; 1992.)

FIG VI-7—Goniophoto of an eye with neovascularization of the angle. (Photo courtesy of Tom Richardson, MD.)

FIG VI-8—Goniophoto showing both an area of sheetlike PAS (left) and open angle (right).

If the ciliary body separates from the scleral spur (cyclodialysis), it will appear gonioscopically as a deep angle recess with a gap between the sclera and the ciliary body. Detecting a very small cleft may require ultrasound biomicroscopy. Figure VI-9 illustrates the variety of gonioscopic findings caused by blunt trauma.

Campbell DG. A comparison of diagnostic techniques in angle-closure glaucoma. *Am J Ophthalmol.* 1979;88:197–204.

Fellman RL, Spaeth GL, Starita RJ. Gonioscopy: key to successful management of glaucoma. In: *Focal Points: Clinical Modules for Ophthalmologists.* San Francisco: American Academy of Ophthalmology; 1984;2:7.

The Optic Nerve

Anatomy and Pathology

The optic nerve head is composed of neural tissue, glial and collagenous supportive tissue, and blood vessels. The optic nerve contains approximately 1.2 million axons. The cell bodies of these axons lie in the ganglion cell layer of the retina. The axons are separated into fascicles by astrocytes. The average diameter of the intraocular portion of the nerve is 1.5 mm.

The retinal ganglion cells are currently divided into two classes, *magnocellular (M) cells* and *parvocellular (P) cells.* The M cells have large-diameter axons, synapse in the magnocellular layer of the lateral geniculate body, and are sensitive to luminance changes in dim illumination. The P cells have smaller-diameter axons and synapse in the parvocellular layers of the lateral geniculate body. They subserve color and fine detail. Most of the ganglion cells are P cells.

The distribution of nerve fibers as they enter the optic nerve head is presented in Figure VI-10. The arcuate nerve fibers entering the superior and inferior poles of the disc seem to be more susceptible to glaucomatous damage. This susceptibility explains the frequent occurrence of arcuate nerve fiber bundle field defects in glaucoma. The pattern of visual field loss is determined by the arrangement of the axons in the optic nerve head.

The optic nerve head can be divided into four layers: the nerve fiber, prelaminar, laminar, and retrolaminar layers (Fig VI-11). The most superficial, the *nerve fiber layer,* can be viewed with the ophthalmoscope using the green filter (red-free ophthalmoscopy). This tissue is supported by astrocytes and receives its vascular supply from the central retinal artery.

The second layer of the nerve head, the *prelaminar layer,* is seen clinically only in the area of the central optic cup. This layer receives the axons of the optic nerve as they angle posteriorly from the plane of the retina to the plane of the choroid. The blood supply of the prelaminar layer comes from the short posterior ciliary arteries.

The short posterior ciliary artery branches in the optic nerve differ from the branches in the choriocapillaris in three ways: they are surrounded by pericytes, they lack fenestrations, and they have tight junctions. That is, they resemble central nervous system and retinal capillaries. They autoregulate and have a blood–brain barrier (Fig VI-12).

The third layer, the *laminar layer,* is a fenestrated area of connective tissue that allows nerve fibers to exit from the eye. Histologically, the lamina cribrosa appears as a series of approximately 10 stacked plates of fenestrated connective tissue whose septae contain small blood vessels. The gray dots that can sometimes be seen ophthalmoscopically in the depths of the optic cup are the superficial openings of the

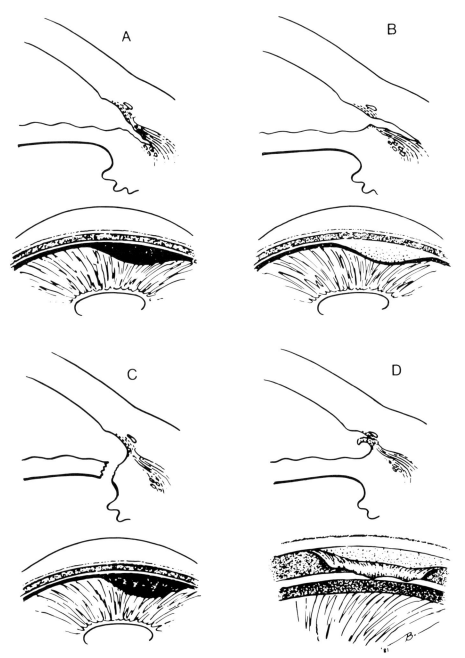

FIG VI-9—Forms of anterior chamber angle injury associated with blunt trauma, showing cross-sectional and corresponding gonioscopic appearance. *A,* Angle recession (tear between longitudinal and circular muscles of ciliary body). *B,* Cyclodialysis (separation of ciliary body from scleral spur) with widening of suprachoroidal space. *C,* Iridodialysis (tear in root of iris). *D,* Trabecular damage (tear in anterior portion of meshwork, creating a flap that is hinged at the scleral spur). (Reproduced with permission from Shields MB. *Textbook of Glaucoma.* 3rd ed. Baltimore: Williams & Wilkins; 1992.)

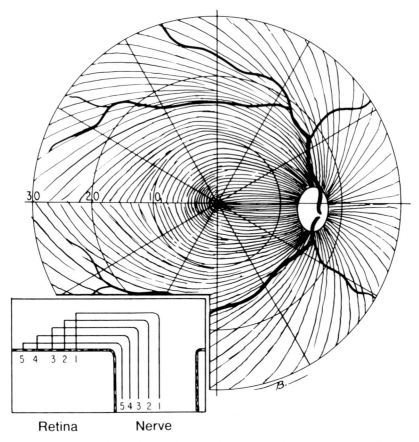

Retina   Nerve

FIG VI-10—Anatomy of retinal nerve fiber distribution. Inset depicts cross-sectional view of axonal arrangement. Peripheral fibers run closer to choroid and exit in periphery of optic nerve, while fibers originating closer to the nerve head are situated closer to the vitreous and occupy a more central portion of the nerve. (Reproduced with permission from Shields MB. *Textbook of Glaucoma.* 3rd ed. Baltimore: Williams & Wilkins; 1992.)

lamina. In hyperopic eyes the lamina cribrosa is approximately 0.7 mm posterior to the retinal plane, whereas in myopic eyes it is half that distance. The vascular supply to the laminar region also comes from the short posterior ciliary arteries.

The *retrolaminar portion* of the optic nerve extends posteriorly from the lamina cribrosa. Thus, it lies outside the globe. The addition of the myelin sheath produced by oligodendrocytes doubles the diameter of the nerve. The vascular supply to the retrolaminar nerve comes from branches of the meningeal arteries and centrifugal branches of the central retinal artery.

On a histological level, early glaucomatous cupping consists of loss of axons, blood vessels, and glial cells. The loss of tissue seems to start at the level of the lamina cribrosa and is associated with compaction and fusion of the laminar plates. It is most pronounced at the superior and inferior poles of the disc. Disc changes may precede detectable visual field loss.

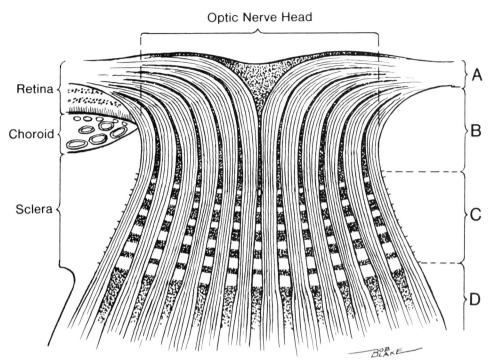

FIG VI-11—Divisions of the optic nerve head. *A*, Surface nerve fiber layer. *B*, Prelaminar region. *C*, Lamina cribrosa region. *D*, Retrolaminar region. (Reproduced with permission from Shields MB. *Textbook of Glaucoma*. 3rd ed. Baltimore: Williams & Wilkins; 1992.)

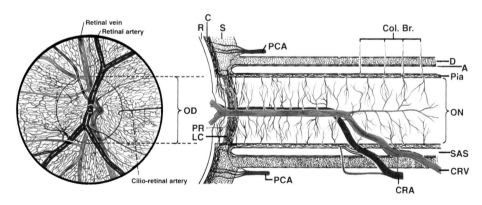

FIG VI-12—Diagrammatic representation of blood supply of the optic nerve head and intraorbital optic nerve. *A*, Arachnoid; *C*, Choroid; *CRA*, Central retinal artery; *Col Br*, Collateral branches; *CRV*, Central retinal vein; *D*, Dura; *LC*, Lamina cribosa; *OD*, Optic disc; *ON*, Optic nerve; *PCA*, Posterior ciliary arteries; *PR*, Prelaminar region; *R*, Retina; *S*, Sclera; *SAS*, Subarachnoid space. (Reproduced by permission from Hayreh SS. Anatomy and physiology of the optic nerve head. *Trans Am Acad Ophthalmol Otolaryngol*. 1974;78:240–254.)

Tissue destruction in more advanced glaucoma extends behind the cribriform plate, and the lamina bows backward. The optic nerve head takes on an excavated and undermined appearance that has been likened to a bean pot.

Glaucomatous cupping in infants and children is accompanied by an expansion of the entire scleral ring. This may explain why cupping seems to occur earlier in children and why reversibility of cupping is more prominent with successful treatment in these cases. Cupping may be reversed in adults as well, but such reversal is less frequent and more subtle.

Theories of Glaucomatous Damage

Elevated IOP is an etiological factor in glaucomatous cupping. Unilateral secondary glaucoma, experimentally induced glaucoma, and observations of the effect of lowering IOP in patients with glaucoma all point to this conclusion. But it is also clear that factors other than pressure can contribute to a given individual's susceptibility to glaucomatous damage. Such factors might include myopia, diabetes, and cardiovascular disease. Because IOP is the only treatable risk factor definitely identified, theories of glaucomatous damage focus on the possible effects of IOP.

It has become common to discuss the theories of glaucomatous damage as if they fell into two categories, mechanical and ischemic. The mechanical theory stressed the importance of direct compression of the optic nerve fibers against the lamina cribrosa with interruption of axoplasmic flow, while the ischemic theory stressed the possible effects of IOP on the blood supply to the nerve. Current thinking regarding glaucomatous damage recognizes that a variety of both vascular and mechanical factors probably combine to damage the optic nerve at the lamina.

A recent theory of particular interest suggests that a disturbance of autoregulation may contribute to nerve damage. The optic nerve vessels normally increase or decrease their tone to maintain a constant blood flow independent of IOP. A disturbance in autoregulation might cause the blood flow in the optic nerve to decrease with increased IOP. Such hypothetical derangement could be related to abnormal vessels or to circulating vasoactive substances, for example.

Examination of the Optic Nerve Head

The optic disc can be examined clinically with a direct ophthalmoscope, an indirect ophthalmoscope, or a slit lamp using a posterior-pole lens. The *direct ophthalmoscope* is often used for disc examination. When used with a red-free filter, it provides a view of the nerve fiber layer of the posterior pole. However, the direct ophthalmoscope does not provide sufficient stereoscopic detail to detect subtle changes in optic disc topography. The *indirect ophthalmoscope* is used for examining the optic disc in young children, uncooperative patients, highly myopic individuals, and individuals with substantial opacities of the media. The view obtained usually suggests both less cupping and less pallor than do slit-lamp methods. The best method of examination for the diagnosis of glaucoma is the *slit lamp combined with a Hruby lens,* a posterior-pole contact lens, or a 60-, 78-, or 90-diopter lens. This system provides high magnification, excellent illumination, and a stereoscopic view of the disc. The slit beam, rather than diffuse illumination, is useful for determining subtle changes in the contour of the nerve head.

Clinical Evaluation of the Optic Nerve Head

The *optic disc* is usually round or slightly oval in shape, and it contains a central *cup*. The tissue between the cup and the disc margin is called the *neural rim*. In normal patients, the rim has a uniform width and a color that ranges from orange to pink.

The size of the physiologic cup is genetically determined and is related to the size of the disc. For a given number of nerve fibers, the larger the overall disc area, the larger the cup. Cup/disc ratio may increase slightly with age. Although there is substantial overlap, nonglaucomatous black individuals have, on the average, larger disc areas and larger cup/disc ratios than do whites. Myopes have larger eyes and larger discs and cups than do emmetropes and hyperopes.

Differentiating physiologic or normal cupping from acquired glaucomatous cupping of the optic disc can be difficult. The early changes of glaucomatous *optic neuropathy* are very subtle (Table VI-2); they include

□ Generalized enlargement of the cup

□ Focal enlargement of the cup

□ Superficial splinter hemorrhage

□ Loss of nerve fiber layer

□ Asymmetry of cupping between the patient's two eyes

Generalized enlargement of the cup may be the earliest change detected in glaucoma. This enlargement may be difficult to appreciate unless previous photographs or diagrams are available. It is useful to compare one eye to the fellow eye,

TABLE VI-2

OPHTHALMOSCOPIC SIGNS OF GLAUCOMA

Generalized signs
Large optic cup
Asymmetry of the cups
Progressive enlargement of the cup

Focal signs
Narrowing (notching) of the rim
Vertical elongation of the cup
Cupping to the rim margin
Regional pallor
Splinter hemorrhage
Nerve fiber layer loss

Less specific signs
Exposed lamina cribrosa
Nasal displacement of vessels
Baring of circumlinear vessels
Peripapillary crescent

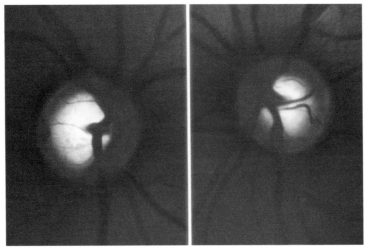

FIG VI-13—Asymmetry of optic discs. The right disc (*left photo*) is distinctly more cupped than the left disc (*right photo*).

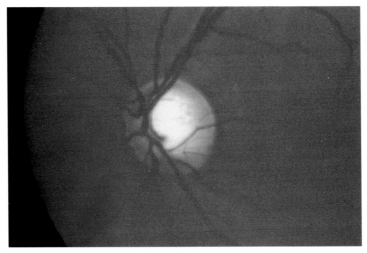

FIG VI-14—Vertical elongation of the cup in a person with glaucoma.

because disc asymmetry is unusual in normal individuals (Fig VI-13). Examination of other family members may clarify whether a large cup is inherited or acquired.

Focal enlargement of the cup appears as localized notching or narrowing of the rim. If this occurs at either (or both) the superior or inferior pole of the disc, the cup becomes vertically oval (Fig VI-14).

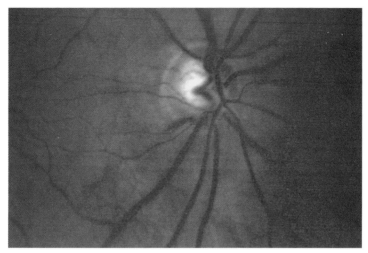

FIG VI-15—Splinter hemorrhage of optic disc at 7 o'clock.

Splinter hemorrhage usually appears as a linear red streak on or near the disc surface (Fig VI-15). The hemorrhage clears over several weeks to months but is often followed by localized notching and pallor of the rim and visual field loss. Some glaucoma patients have repeated episodes of optic disc hemorrhage, while others have none. Individuals with normal-tension glaucoma are particularly likely to have disc hemorrhages. Optic disc hemorrhage is an important prognostic sign for the development or progression of visual field loss. Any patient with an optic disc hemorrhage requires detailed evaluation and follow-up.

Glaucomatous optic atrophy is associated with loss of axons in the nerve fiber layer. In the normal eye the nerve fiber layer may best be visualized with red-free illumination; it appears as a pattern of striations that radiate toward the optic disc. With the development of glaucoma, the nerve fiber layer thins and becomes less visible. The loss may be diffuse (generalized) or localized to specific bundles (Fig VI-16). The nerve fiber layer can be seen most clearly in high-contrast black-and-white photographs, and experienced observers may recognize even early disease if good-quality photos are available.

Other less specific signs of glaucomatous damage include nasal displacement of the vessels and baring of the circumlinear vessels. With advanced damage the cup becomes pale and markedly excavated.

A number of sophisticated image analysis systems have been developed to evaluate the optic disc. These machines give quantitative measurements of various parameters, including cup volume and neuroretinal rim area. No system is currently more useful than good-quality photographs. Image analysis systems are expected to undergo further development and to be utilized widely in the diagnosis and management of glaucoma patients.

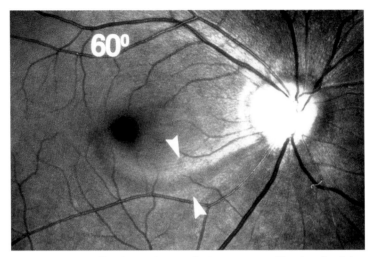

FIG VI-16—Nerve fiber layer photograph shows a nerve fiber bundle defect (arrowheads).

Recording of Optic Nerve Findings

It is common practice to grade an optic disc by comparing the diameter of the cup to the diameter of the disc. This ratio is usually expressed as a decimal such as 0.2, but such a description poorly conveys the appearance of the nerve head. To avoid confusion, the examiner must specify whether the cup is being defined by the change in color or in contour between the central area of the disc and the surrounding rim. Furthermore, the examiner must specify what is being measured—the horizontal diameter, the vertical diameter, or the longest diameter of the disc. It is more descriptive if the dimensions of the cup are specified by both color and contour criteria in the vertical and horizontal meridians. The rim, which contains the neural elements, should be described in detail; color, width, focal thinning or pallor, and slope should all be included. There is a correlation between the rim area and the size of optic disc; i.e., larger optic discs have larger rim areas.

The best record of the optic disc is a photograph, preferably stereoscopic and magnified. This record allows the examiner to compare the present status of the patient to the baseline status without resorting to memory or grading systems. Moreover, photos allow better evaluation when a patient has changed doctors. Sometimes subtle optic disc changes become apparent when the clinician compares one set of photographs to a previous set. Careful diagrams of the optic nerve head are useful when photography is not available.

The Visual Field

The goal of glaucoma management is the preservation of visual function. Visual function, a very complex concept, can be measured in a variety of ways. For many years the standard measurement has been clinical perimetry, which measures differ-

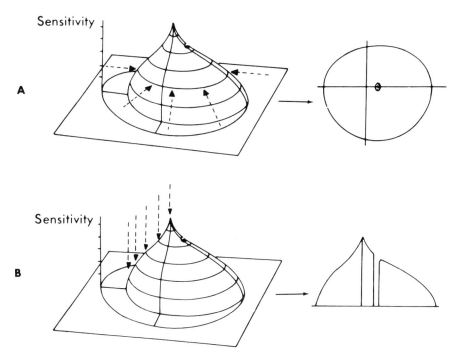

FIG VI-17—*A*, Isopter (kinetic) perimetry. Test object of fixed intensity is moved along several meridians toward fixation. Points where the object is first perceived are plotted in a circle. *B*, Static perimetry. Stationary test object is increased in intensity from below threshold until perceived by the patient. Threshold values yield a graphic profile section. (Reproduced with permission from Kolker AE, Hetherington J, eds. *Becker-Shaffer's Diagnosis and Therapy of the Glaucomas*. 5th ed. St Louis: CV Mosby Co; 1983. Modified from Aulhorn E, Harms H. In: Leydhecker W. *Glaucoma*. Tutzing Symposium. Basel: S Karger; 1967.)

ential light sensitivity, or the ability of the subject to distinguish a stimulus light from background illumination. As usually performed in glaucoma examinations, the test uses white light and measures what is conventionally referred to as the *visual field*. The classic description of the visual field given by Harry Moss Traquair (1875–1954), is "an island hill of vision in a sea of darkness." The island of vision is usually described as a three-dimensional graphic representation of differential light sensitivity at different positions in space (Fig VI-17).

Perimetry refers to the clinical assessment of the visual field. Perimetry has traditionally served two major purposes in the management of glaucoma: the identification of abnormal fields and the quantitative assessment of normal or abnormal fields to guide follow-up care. It has been accepted practice to use the same type of test for both purposes.

More recently, a variety of methods have been introduced to test visual functions other than differential light sensitivity. The general clinical utility of these newer tests has not been established. It is likely that in different individuals, different tests will show abnormalities at different times. Some methods may be better for identification than for follow-up of defects, and vice versa. If, for example, it is true that M cells are selectively damaged early in glaucoma, tests that measure M cell function would perhaps be used for identification of early glaucoma. For the immediate future, however, differential light perimetry with white light will almost certainly continue to be the standard method of identification and follow-up. Other measurements of function that are being investigated and may find a clinical place in the future include the following:

☐ *Blue/yellow perimetry.* Standard projection perimeters can be modified to project a blue stimulus onto a yellow background. This method seems to be sensitive in the early identification of glaucomatous damage.

☐ *Contrast sensitivity.* This test measures a subject's ability to detect a pattern of alternating light and dark bands presented at varying frequencies and degrees of contrast.

☐ *Flicker sensitivity.* This test measures the ability of the subject to recognize the difference between a flickering light from one that is constantly on. The contrast can be varied.

☐ *Visual evoked potentials (VEP)* and *electroretinography (ERG).* Cortical (VEP) or retinal (ERG) electrical responses to a stimulus, such as a reversing pattern of light and dark squares or a flickering light, are recorded. Although these tests require visual attention, they do not require a subjective response.

Clinical Perimetry

The two major types of perimetry in general use today are manual kinetic and static perimetry using a Goldmann-type bowl perimeter and automated static perimetry using a bowl perimeter. Other methods are discussed in standard perimetric texts. In the United States the predominant automated static perimeter is currently the Humphrey Visual Field Analyzer. Most of the clinical examples given are from Humphrey perimeters, and the descriptions apply most directly to that instrument. However, the principles apply to a number of other excellent instruments.

The following are brief definitions of some of the major perimetric terms:

☐ *Threshold.* The differential light sensitivity at which a stimulus of given size and duration of presentation is seen 50% of the time—in practice, the dimmest spot detected during testing.

☐ *Suprathreshold.* Above the threshold; it is generally used to mean brighter-than-threshold stimulus. A stimulus may also be made suprathreshold by increasing the size or duration of presentation.

☐ *Kinetic testing.* Perimetry in which a target is moved from a nonseeing area toward a seeing area until it is just seen. In general practice, kinetic perimetry is usually performed manually by a perimetrist who chooses the target, moves it, and records the results.

☐ *Static testing.* In static perimetry a stationary stimulus is presented at various locations. The intensity and duration of the stimulus can be varied at each location to determine the threshold. Although static perimetry may be done manually, and is often combined with manual kinetic perimetry, in current practice the term usually refers to automated perimetry.

□ *Isopter.* A line on a visual field representation—usually on a two-dimensional sheet of paper—connecting points with the same threshold.

□ *Depression.* A decrease in sensitivity.

□ *Scotoma.* An area of decreased sensitivity within the visual field surrounded by an area of greater sensitivity.

□ *Decibel.* A 0.1 log unit. This is a relative term used in both kinetic and static perimetry that has no absolute value. Its value depends on the maximum illumination of the perimeter. As usually used, it refers to log units of attenuation of the maximum intensity.

Patterns of Glaucomatous Nerve Loss

The hallmark defect of glaucoma is the nerve fiber bundle defect that results from damage at the optic nerve head. The pattern of nerve fibers in the retinal area served by the damaged nerve fiber bundle will correspond to the specific defect. The common names for the classic visual field defects are derived from their appearance as plotted on a kinetic visual field chart. In static perimetry, however, the sample points are in a grid pattern; thus, the representation of visual field defects on a static perimetry chart generally lacks the smooth contours suggested by such terms as *arcuate.*

The following are the typical glaucomatous defects that are shown in Figures VI-18 through VI-21:

□ Paracentral scotoma

□ Arcuate or Bjerrum scotoma

□ Nasal step

□ Temporal wedge

Glaucoma that is far advanced may leave merely a central island of vision (Fig VI-22).

The superior and inferior poles of the optic nerve appear to be most susceptible to glaucomatous damage. Damage to small scattered bundles throughout the optic nerve head will produce a generalized decrease in sensitivity, which is harder to recognize than focal defects.

Variables in Perimetry

Perimetry, whether automated or manual, is subject to a variety of variables, the most important of which are the following:

□ *Patient.* Humans vary in their attentiveness and response time from day to day. In addition, retinal sensitivity appears to vary both over time and, particularly, in abnormal areas.

□ *Perimetrist.* The perimetrist performing manual perimetry will administer the test slightly differently at different times. Different technicians or physicians will also vary from one another.

□ *Fixation.* If the eye is slightly torted or if the patient is fixing off center, the defect may shift. Especially in automated static tests (because the test logic does not change), a defect may thus appear and disappear.

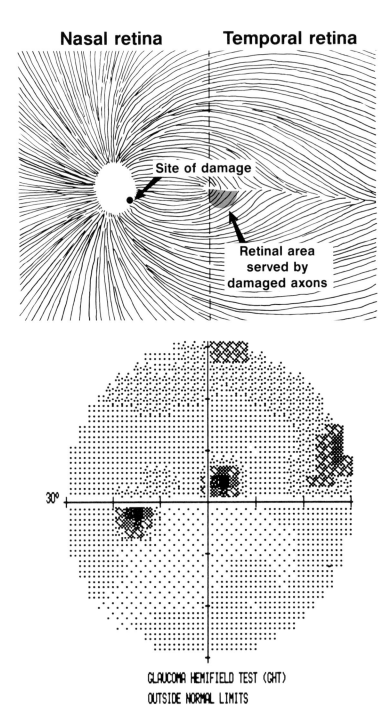

Nasal retina　　**Temporal retina**

Site of damage

Retinal area
served by
damaged axons

30°

GLAUCOMA HEMIFIELD TEST (GHT)
OUTSIDE NORMAL LIMITS

FIG VI-18—Paracentral scotoma. Loss of nerve fibers from the inferior pole, originating from the infer-otemporal retina, resulted in the superonasal scotoma shown. A paracentral scotoma is an island of relative or absolute visual loss within 10° of fixation. Paracentral scotomata may be single, as in this case, or multiple, and they may occur as isolated findings or may be associated with other early defects (Humphrey 30-2 program).

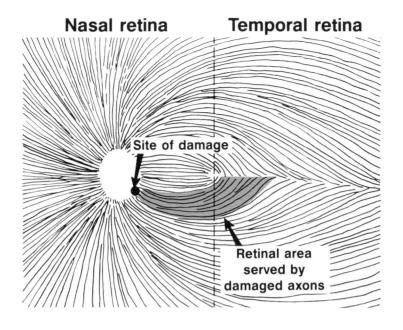

Nasal retina   **Temporal retina**

Site of damage

Retinal area
served by
damaged axons

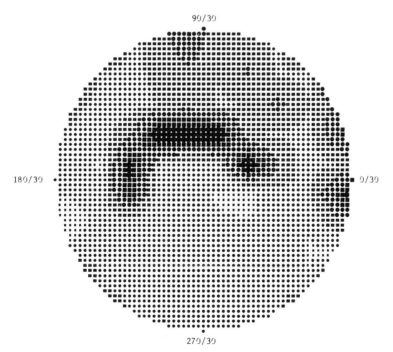

FIG VI-19—Arcuate Bjerrum scotoma. Glaucomatous damage to a nerve fiber bundle that contains axons from both inferonasal and inferotemporal retina resulted in the arcuate defect shown. An arcuate scotoma occurs in the area 10°–20° from fixation. The scotoma often begins as a single area of relative loss, which then becomes larger, deeper, and multifocal. In its full form an arcuate scotoma arches from the blind spot and ends at the nasal raphe, becoming wider and closer to fixation on the nasal side (Octopus 32 program).

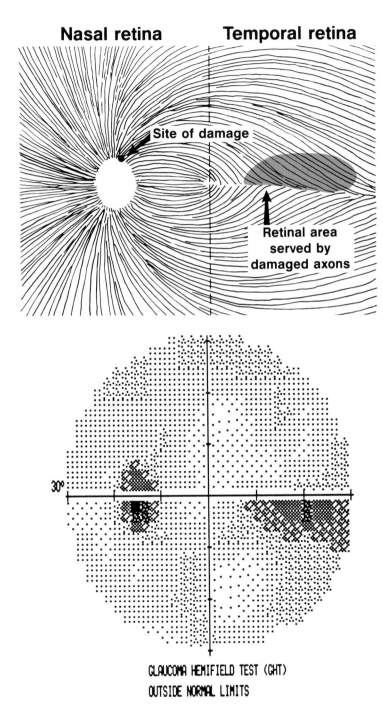

Nasal retina **Temporal retina**

Site of damage

Retinal area
served by
damaged axons

30°

GLAUCOMA HEMIFIELD TEST (GHT)

OUTSIDE NORMAL LIMITS

FIG VI-20—Nasal step. Damage to superior nerve fibers serving the superotemporal retina beyond the paracentral area resulted in this nasal step. A nasal step is a relative depression of one horizontal hemifield compared to the other. In kinetic perimetry it is defined as a discontinuity or depression in one or more nasal isopters near the horizontal raphe (Humphrey 30-2 program).

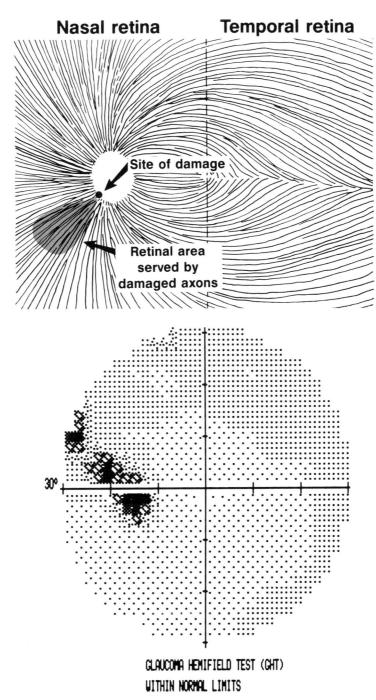

Nasal retina **Temporal retina**

Site of damage

Retinal area
served by
damaged axons

30°

GLAUCOMA HEMIFIELD TEST (GHT)
WITHIN NORMAL LIMITS

FIG VI-21—Temporal wedge defect. Damage to the nerve fiber bundle in the inferonasal nerve serving the retina superotemporal to the blind spot produced this temporal wedge. Note that the hemifield test is normal; the test does not include points temporal to the disc. A temporal wedge, also called a temporal step, is a wedge-shaped defect that extends temporally from the blind spot or extends from the periphery toward the blind spot. This term is not used to describe defects that extend from the point of fixation or appear to point toward fixation (Humphrey 30-2 program).

Symb.	dB	asb
⋮⋮	51–36	0.008–0.25
⋮⋮	35–31	0.31–0.8
⋮⋮	30–26	1–2.5
⋮⋮	25–21	3.1–8
▪▪	20–16	10–25
▪▪	15–11	31–80
▪▪	10–6	100–250
▪	5–1	315–800
■	0	1000

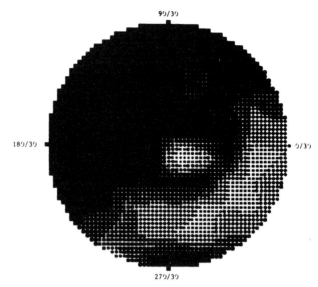

FIG VI-22—Examination of the right eye shows dense nasal loss and dense superior loss. Remaining but depressed field is seen inferiorly, superotemporally, and a small island can be seen centrally (Octopus 32 program). (Reproduced with permission from Silverstone DE, Hirsch J. *Automated Visual Field Testing. Techniques of Examination and Interpretation.* East Norwalk, CT: Appleton-Century-Crofts; 1986.)

□ *Background luminance.* The luminance of the surface onto which the perimetric stimulus is projected affects retinal sensitivity and thus the hill of vision. Clinical perimetry is usually done with a background luminance of 4.0–31.5 apostilbs, in the low photopic range. Here sensitivity is greatest at fixation and falls steadily toward the periphery.

□ *Stimulus luminance.* For a given stimulus size and presentation time, the brighter it is, the more visible it is.

□ *Size of stimulus.* For a given brightness and duration of presentation, the larger the stimulus, the more likely it is to be perceived. The sizes of standard stimuli are: $0 = 1/16 \text{ mm}^2$, $I = 1/4 \text{ mm}^2$, $II = 1 \text{ mm}^2$, $III = 4 \text{ mm}^2$, $IV = 16 \text{ mm}^2$, $V = 64 \text{ mm}^2$.

□ *Presentation time.* Up to about 0.2 second, the longer the presentation time, the more visible a given stimulus.

□ *Patient refraction.* Uncorrected refractive errors cause blurring on the retina and decrease the visibility of stimuli. To focus the fixation point the patient's refractive error must be compensated for according to the depth of the perimeter bowl.

□ *Pupil size.* Pupil size affects the amount of light entering the eye, and it should be recorded on each field. Testing with pupils smaller than 3 mm in diameter may induce artifacts. Pupil size should be kept constant from test to test.

□ *Wavelength of background and stimulus.* As noted above, color perimetry may yield different results from white-on-white perimetry.

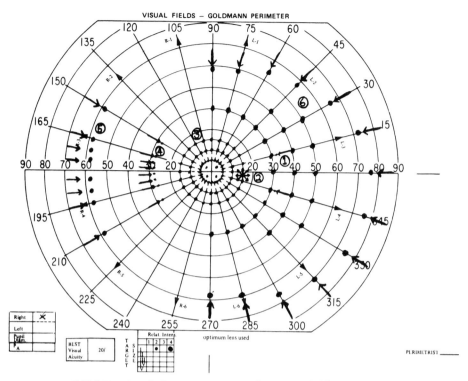

FIG VI-23—Armaly-Drance screening technique on Goldmann perimeter.

□ *Speed of stimulus movement.* If a kinetic target is moved quickly, it may have gone well beyond the location at which it is first seen by the time the patient responds.

Manual Perimetry

The two goals of perimetry—to identify abnormalities and to define and record visual function for comparison over time—are most commonly pursued using the *Armaly-Drance screening technique.* This screening technique for the detection of early glaucomatous visual field loss was originally developed for the Goldmann perimeter but has been adapted for a number of instruments. It combines a kinetic examination of the peripheral isopters with a suprathreshold static examination of the central field (Fig VI-23).

With this technique the kinetic perimeter is used to determine the stimulus that is just suprathreshold for the central 25°—usually the Goldmann I–2e. The central isopter is then plotted kinetically with this stimulus to detect nasal, temporal, or vertical steps, with special attention paid to the 15° straddling the horizontal and vertical meridians. The blind spot is mapped with the same stimulus moving from the center of the blind spot outward in eight directions. The same stimulus is then used

53

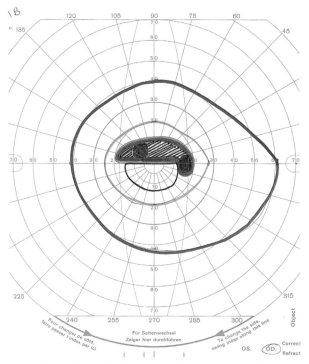

FIG VI-24—Split fixation (Goldmann perimeter).

in static presentations to search for paracentral and arcuate defects. A more intense stimulus, often the equivalent of a Goldmann I–4e, is used to search for both nasal step and temporal sector defects to prepare a kinetic plot of the peripheral isopter.

A different perimetric technique must be used for quantifying defects and for following patients with established glaucomatous damage. This form of perimetry quantifies visual field defects by size, shape, and depth and determines whether the disease is progressing or not. If the examiner is using a kinetic technique, targets of different size and brightness must be employed. The technique of quantifying defects with kinetic perimetry is well described in standard texts. An example of a quantified defect is shown in Figure VI-24.

Anderson DR. *Perimetry With and Without Automation.* St Louis: CV Mosby Co; 1987.

Progression of glaucomatous field loss generally occurs in areas damaged previously. Scotomata become larger and deeper, and new scotomata appear in the same hemifield. Arcuate scotomata extend to the peripheral boundaries on the nasal side; they break through to the periphery. The ophthalmologist who quantifies defects with precision can use this pattern of progression to determine a patient's ongoing stability or progression.

Since high-quality manual threshold perimetry requires a well-trained and conscientious perimetrist, and even the best perimetrist varies from day to day, computerized, or automated, field testing has become increasingly widespread over the past decade. Computerized static perimetry has shown itself to be at least as good as the best-quality manual perimetry in the detection and quantification of glaucomatous defects. Manual perimetry, however, is probably more helpful in monitoring end-stage visual field loss.

Automated Static Perimetry

A computerized perimeter must be able to determine threshold sensitivity at multiple points in the visual field, to perform an adequate test in a reasonable amount of time, and to present results in a comprehensible form. The best instruments currently available are bowl perimeters that project stimuli in programmed locations. The intensity of the stimulus is varied by a system of filters that attenuate the stimulus, usually allowing measurement to approximately 1 decibel (dB).

Three general categories of testing strategy are currently in common use:

□ *Suprathreshold testing.* A stimulus, usually one expected to be a little brighter than threshold, is presented at various locations and recorded as seen or not seen. Sometimes, if it is not seen, it is presented again, and if not seen a second time, is recorded as not seen. Then the stimulus may be presented at maximum brightness to determine if a defect is relative or absolute. This type of test is designed to detect moderate to severe defects.

□ *Threshold-related strategy.* At a few points, the threshold is determined and a presumed hill of vision is extrapolated from these points. Then a stimulus 4–6 dB brighter is presented, and the results are recorded as either seen or not seen. This type of test will detect moderate to severe defects, but it may miss mild defects (Fig VI-25).

□ *Threshold.* Threshold testing is the current standard for automated perimetry in glaucoma management. Threshold is determined by a bracketing strategy. Usually, several points are tested twice to determine a patient's variability, and occasional tests are done to monitor fixation and to assess the frequency of a given individual's false-positive and false-negative responses (Fig VI-26).

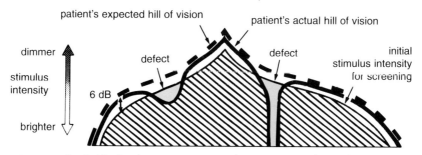

FIG VI-25—Threshold-related screening strategy. This strategy records tested points as seen or not seen. Screening is done at an intensity 6 dB brighter than the expected threshold, and points missed twice at that level are recorded as defects. (Reproduced with permission from *The Field Analyzer Primer.* San Leandro, CA: Allergan Humphrey; 1989.)

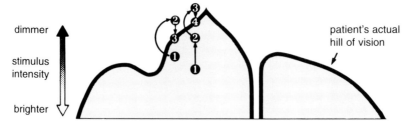

FIG VI-26—Full-threshold strategy. This strategy determines retinal sensitivity at each tested point by altering the stimulus intensity in 4-dB steps until the threshold is crossed. It then recrosses the threshold, moving in 2-dB steps, in order to check and refine the accuracy of the measurement. (Reproduced with permission from *The Field Analyzer Primer.* San Leandro, CA: Allergan Humphrey; 1989.)

Test Types and Applications

Of the many tests available, only a few are generally used in glaucoma management.

Screening tests Screening tests may or may not be threshold-related, and they cover varying areas of the visual field. Suprathreshold tests are not recommended for glaucoma suspects, since they do not provide a good reference for future comparison. These tests are appropriate for screening people not suspected of having glaucoma. On a full-field screening test such as the Octopus 07 or Humphrey full-field 120-point test, a field should be considered abnormal if more than 10 points are missed or if 2 or more adjacent points are missed. A threshold field should be performed on such patients unless a cause other than glaucoma is apparent on examination.

Threshold tests The most common programs for glaucoma testing are the central 24° and 30° programs such as the Octopus 32 and the Humphrey 24-2 and 30-2 (Fig VI-27). These programs test the central field using a 6° grid. They test points 3° above and 3° below the horizontal midline and facilitate diagnosis of defects that respect this line.

Although a 30°–60° program is available on most static threshold perimeters, it is usually not performed. The abandonment of peripheral testing that has accompanied the shift from manual to automated perimetry is the subject of ongoing discussion, but after a decade of static threshold perimetry, there is no trend to move beyond the central program. In part, at least, this pattern of use is related to a subtle change in the role of the visual field examination. The automated static threshold field determines retinal sensitivity at a preset series of points. If a defect is found, it is not plotted precisely as it would be with manual perimetry. Ideally, an abnormal field is repeated, and the result is a precise map of sensitivity at selected locations. In practice, this method appears to be superior to kinetic testing for following a patient over time.

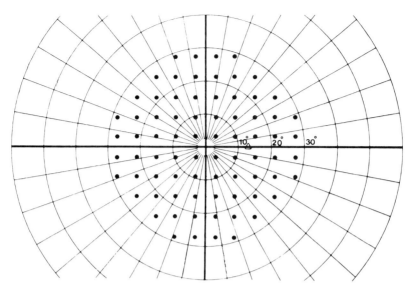

FIG VI-27—Central 30-2 threshold test pattern, right eye. (Reproduced with permission from *The Field Analyzer Primer.* San Leandro, CA: Allergan Humphrey; 1989.)

Interpretation of a Single Field

Quality   The quality of the field should be evaluated first. The percentage of fixation losses, false positives and false negatives, and the fluctuations of doubly determined points are assessed. Damaged areas of the field are more variable than normal areas. Glaucomatous damage may cause an increase in false-negative responses unrelated to patient reliability. In general, the average fluctuation between two determinations should be less than 2 dB in a normal field, less than 3 dB in a field with early damage, and less than 4 dB in a field with moderate damage. After testing a badly damaged visual field, it is helpful to look at the least damaged areas to determine how reliable the patient was in those areas.

Normality or abnormality   Next, the normality or abnormality should be assessed. Normal fields are most sensitive centrally under photopic conditions, and sensitivity falls steadily toward the periphery. A cluster of two or more points depressed ≥5 dB compared to surrounding points is suspicious. A single point depressed >10 dB is very unusual but is of less value on a single visual field than a cluster, because cluster points confirm one another. Corresponding points above and below the horizontal midline should not vary markedly; normally the superior field is depressed 1–2 dB compared to the inferior field.

To aid the clinician in interpreting the numerical data generated by threshold tests, field indices have been developed by perimeter manufacturers. In addition to the mean difference from normal and the test-retest variability, other measures of the irregularity of the visual field include Humphrey pattern standard deviation and Octopus loss variance indices. These indices highlight localized depressions in the field. When corrected for short-term fluctuation, the indices are termed *corrected pattern standard deviation* and *corrected loss variance.*

These indices help to distinguish between generalized field depression and localized loss. An abnormally high pattern standard deviation indicates that some points of the visual field are depressed relative to other points in the field after correction for the patient's moment-to-moment variability. Such a finding is suggestive of focal damage such as that occurring with glaucoma (and many other conditions). A normal pattern standard deviation in an eye with an abnormal visual field indicates a generalized depression of the hill of vision such as that occurring with media opacity. Such generalized loss may also occur with diffuse glaucomatous damage, and thus an abnormal pattern deviation has greater diagnostic specificity than a generalized loss of sensitivity.

The Humphrey STATPAC 2 program performs an additional calculation on a single field to determine the likelihood that a field shows glaucomatous damage. This test is designed only for glaucoma and involves comparison of corresponding points above and below the horizontal midline (Fig VI-28). The hemifield analysis is at least as accurate as other methods for the classification of single visual fields.

Artifacts Artifacts must be identified. The following are common artifacts seen on automated perimetry:

□ *Lens rim.* The corrective lens is decentered or set too far from the eye; the lens rim may project into the central 30° as shown in Figure VI-29.

□ *Cloverleaf field.* If a patient stops paying attention and ceases to respond partway through a visual field, a distinctive field pattern may develop, depending on the test logic of a given perimeter. Figure VI-30 shows a cloverleaf field, the result of

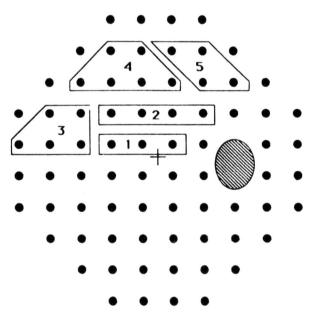

FIG VI-28—Superior field zones used in the glaucoma hemifield test. (Reproduced with permission from *The STATPAC User's Guide.* San Leandro, CA: Allergan Humphrey; 1989.)

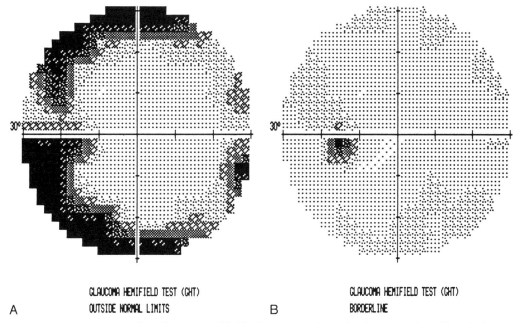

GLAUCOMA HEMIFIELD TEST (GHT)

GLAUCOMA HEMIFIELD TEST (GHT)

OUTSIDE NORMAL LIMITS

GLAUCOMA HEMIFIELD TEST (GHT)

BORDERLINE

A

B

FIG VI-29—Lens rim artifact. The two visual fields shown were obtained 9 days apart. The field on the left, A, shows a typical lens rim artifact, whereas the corrective lens was positioned appropriately for the field on the right, B (Humphrey 30-2 programs).

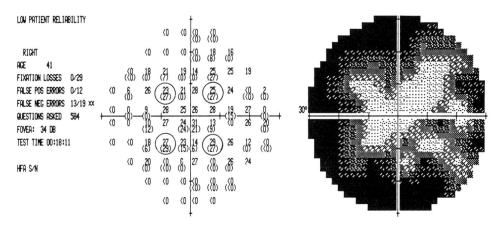

FIG VI-30—Cloverleaf field. The Humphrey visual field perimeter test is designed so that four circled points are checked initially and the testing in each quadrant proceeds outward from these points. If the patient ceases to respond after only a few points have been tested, the result is some variation of the cloverleaf field shown above (Humphrey 30-2 programs).

the test logic of the Humphrey 30-2 perimeter, which begins testing with the points circled and works outward.

☐ *Incorrect corrective lens.* If an incorrect corrective lens is used, the resulting field will be generally depressed. In practice, such an error is rarely noted but probably accounts for occasional inexplicably depressed fields that improve on follow-up testing.

☐ *High false-positive rate.* If a patient inaccurately registers that he or she sees a stimulus, the result may be a field with impossibly high threshold values (Fig VI-31). There will also be a high false-positive and a high fixation-loss rate if the instrument records fixation losses by presenting stimuli in the blind spot. Careful instruction of the patient may sometimes resolve this artifact.

Interpretation of a Series of Fields

Interpretation of serial visual fields should meet two goals: separating real change from ordinary variation and using the information from the field testing to determine the likelihood that a change is related to glaucomatous progression. Statistical programs (the Humphrey STATPAC 2 or Octopus Delta program) are valuable aids in analysis over time, and each is well described in the owner's manual that comes with the program. In the absence of a statistical package, comparison becomes more cumbersome. Whatever method the clinician uses, however, the fundamental requirement for adequate interpretation over time is a good baseline visual field. Often the patient experiences a learning effect, and the second visual field may show substantial improvement over the first (Fig VI-32). At least two visual fields should be obtained as early on in a patient's course as possible and, if they are quite different, a third. Subsequent visual fields should be compared to these baseline fields. A follow-up visual field that appears to be quite different should be repeated for confirmation.

No hard-and-fast rules define what determines visual field progression, but the following are reasonable guidelines:

☐ A cluster of two or more points ≥5 dB below the baseline that are also depressed on a repeat field is probably abnormal.

☐ A single point depressed ≥10 dB that is present on a repeat visual field is probably abnormal.

Cases such as that shown in Figure VI-33 are easy to recognize. A general decrease in sensitivity may be secondary to glaucoma or may be related to media opacity. Clinical correlation is required, which is often difficult. Two causes of general decline in sensitivity that may confuse interpretation are variable miosis (often related to use of eyedrops) and cataract (Fig VI-34). To help avoid this problem, the pupil size should remain constant from field to field if at all possible.

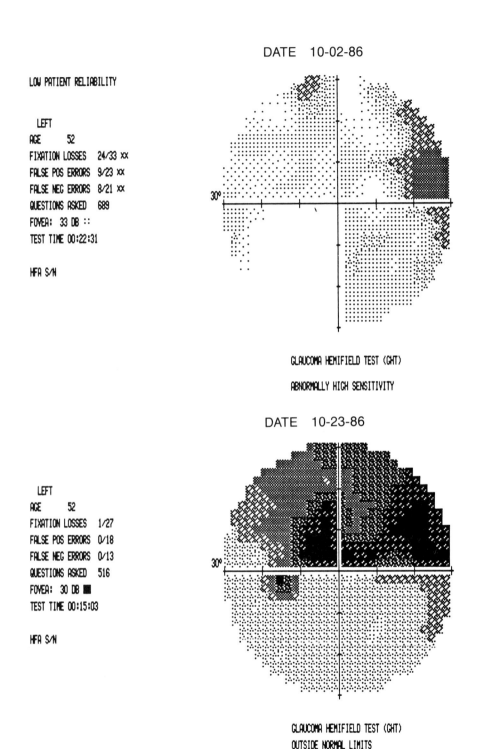

DATE 10-02-86

LEFT
AGE   52
FIXATION LOSSES   24/33 xx
FALSE POS ERRORS 9/23 xx
FALSE NEG ERRORS 8/21 xx
QUESTIONS ASKED   689
FOVEA: 33 DB ::
TEST TIME 00:22:31

HFA S/N

30°

GLAUCOMA HEMIFIELD TEST (GHT)

ABNORMALLY HIGH SENSITIVITY

DATE   10-23-86

LEFT
AGE   52
FIXATION LOSSES   1/27
FALSE POS ERRORS 0/18
FALSE NEG ERRORS 0/13
QUESTIONS ASKED   516
FOVEA: 30 DB ■
TEST TIME 00:15:03

HFA S/N

30°

GLAUCOMA HEMIFIELD TEST (GHT)
OUTSIDE NORMAL LIMITS

FIG VI-31—High false-positive rate. The top visual field contains characteristic "white scotomata," which represent areas of impossibly high retinal sensitivity. Upon return visit 3 weeks later, the patient was carefully instructed to respond only when she saw the light, resulting in the bottom visual field, which shows good reliability and demonstrates the patient's dense superior visual field loss (Humphrey 30-2 programs).

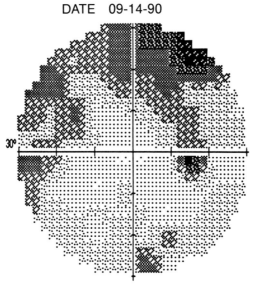

DATE   09-14-90

GLAUCOMA HEMIFIELD TEST (GHT)
OUTSIDE NORMAL LIMITS

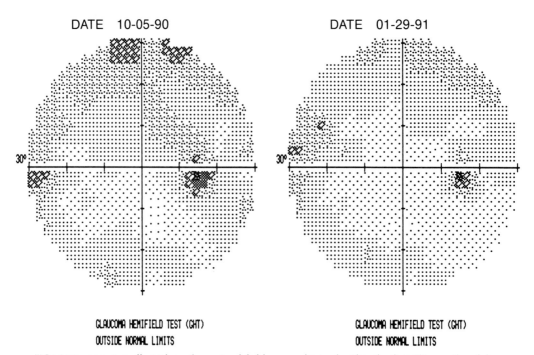

DATE   10-05-90

GLAUCOMA HEMIFIELD TEST (GHT)
OUTSIDE NORMAL LIMITS

DATE   01-29-91

GLAUCOMA HEMIFIELD TEST (GHT)
OUTSIDE NORMAL LIMITS

FIG VI-32—Learning effect. These three visual fields were obtained within the first 3½ months of diagnosis in a patient with very early, clinically stable, glaucoma. They illustrate the learning effect between the first and second visual field. The third field is similar to the second field, and the second and third visual fields were used for subsequent follow-up of the patient (Humphrey 30-2 program).

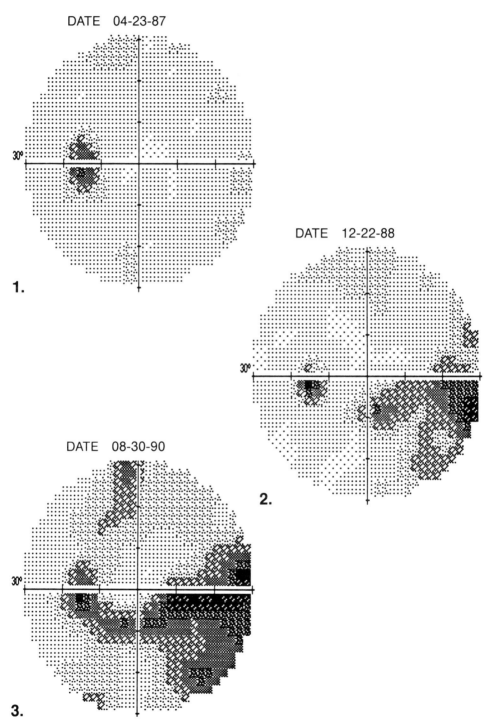

DATE   04-23-87

1.

DATE   12-22-88

2.

DATE   08-30-90

3.

FIG VI-33—Progression of glaucomatous damage. The three fields shown illustrate the development and advancement of a visual field defect. Between the first and second visual fields, the patient developed a significant inferior nasal step. The third visual field illustrates the extension of this defect to the blind spot, as well as the development of superior visual field loss (Humphrey 30-2 program).

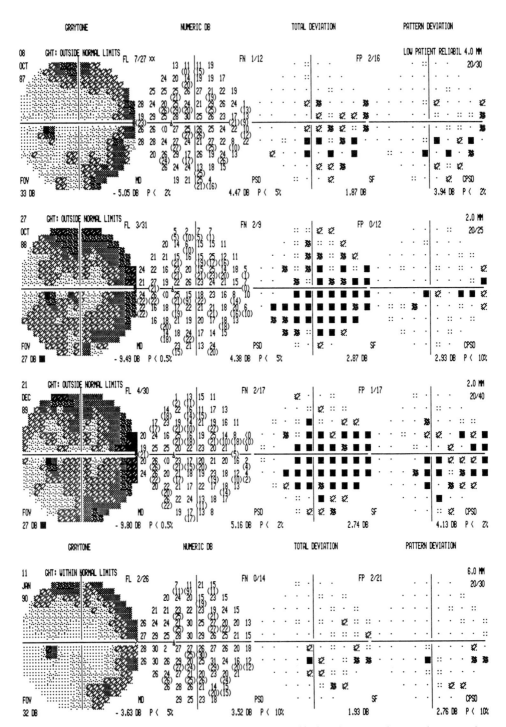

FIG VI-34—Pupil size. The first field in this series was obtained before the patient began pilocarpine therapy. The second and third fields were obtained with a miotic pupil. Before the fourth field was obtained, the patient's pupil was dilated (Humphrey 30-2 program).

It is important to correlate changes in the visual field with the optic disc. If no correlation is evident, other causes of visual loss should be considered, such as ischemic optic neuropathy, demyelinating or other neurologic disease, pituitary tumor, and so on. This consideration is especially important when

☐ The patient's optic disc seems less cupped than would be expected for the degree of field loss

☐ The pallor of the disc is more impressive than the cupping

☐ The progression of the visual field loss seems excessive

☐ The pattern of visual field loss is uncharacteristic for glaucoma, e.g., respecting the vertical midline

Anderson DR. *Automated Static Perimetry.* St Louis: Mosby–Year Book; 1992.

Drake MV. A primer on automated perimetry. In: *Focal Points: Clinical Modules for Ophthalmologists.* San Francisco: American Academy of Ophthalmology; 1993;11:8.

Drance SM, Anderson DR, eds. *Automatic Perimetry in Glaucoma: A Practical Guide.* Orlando, Fla: Grune & Stratton; 1985.

Harrington DO. *The Visual Fields: A Textbook and Atlas of Clinical Perimetry.* 6th ed. St Louis: CV Mosby Co; 1989.

Lieberman MF. Glaucoma and automated perimetry. In: *Focal Points: Clinical Modules for Ophthalmologists.* San Francisco: American Academy of Ophthalmology; 1993;11:9.

Walsh TJ, ed. *Visual Fields: Examination and Interpretation.* Ophthalmology Monograph 3, 2nd ed. San Francisco: American Academy of Ophthalmology; 1996.

CHAPTER VII

Open-Angle Glaucoma

Primary Open-Angle Glaucoma

Primary open-angle glaucoma is a chronic, slowly progressive optic neuropathy characterized by atrophy and cupping of the optic nerve head and associated with characteristic patterns of visual field loss. IOP is an important risk factor for primary open-angle glaucoma, although other factors, many not yet defined, also contribute to the development of this disease.

Epidemiology

Primary open-angle glaucoma is by far the most common type of glaucoma found in the United States. Estimates of its prevalence in the general population 40 years of age or older range from 1.3% to 2.1%. The disease occurs much more frequently in older individuals with a prevalence 3–10 times higher among persons 80 years and older than among persons in their 40s. Blacks are affected more frequently by primary open-angle glaucoma than are whites; its prevalence is estimated as being 3–6 times higher in the black population. The disease occurs at an earlier age and results more commonly in blindness among blacks than among whites. In the United States it is the leading cause of nonreversible blindness among blacks and the third leading cause among whites, following age-related macular degeneration and diabetic retinopathy.

Genetics

Familial factors, many of which remain to be defined, have an important role in an individual's underlying susceptibility to the development of primary open-angle glaucoma. The prevalence of primary open-angle glaucoma is higher among first-degree relatives of subjects with the disease. However, accurate estimates of the exact degree of risk are lacking.

The genetic basis of juvenile-onset glaucoma is better understood than that of primary open-angle glaucoma. An autosomal dominant inheritance pattern has been documented in several large pedigrees, and a genetic marker associated with juvenile-onset glaucoma has been isolated on chromosome 1q. The genetic factors influencing primary open-angle glaucoma appear to be far more complex. A single-gene hypothesis fails to explain the frequent lack of glaucomatous defects in most first-degree relatives of primary open-angle glaucoma patients. The search for genetic markers associated with glaucoma is continuing.

Clinical Features

Primary open-angle glaucoma is usually insidious in onset, slowly progressive, and painless. Because central visual acuity is relatively unaffected until late in the disease, visual loss generally progresses without symptoms. While usually bilateral, the disease can be quite asymmetrical.

Primary open-angle glaucoma has been defined by IOP levels, optic disc appearance, and visual field loss, either singularly or in various combinations. Large, population-based epidemiological studies have revealed a mean IOP of approximately 16 mm Hg, with a standard deviation of approximately 3 mm Hg. The range of normal IOP has been defined as 2 standard deviations above and below the mean IOP, or approximately 10–21 mm Hg.

Intraocular pressure of greater than 21 mm Hg has often been defined as "abnormal," and in many cases, as glaucoma. There are a number of problems with this definition. First, it is now known that IOP in a general population is not represented by a gaussian distribution but is skewed toward higher pressures. Intraocular pressures of 21 mm Hg and above would thus not necessarily represent abnormality from a statistical standpoint. More important, IOP distribution curves in glaucomatous and nonglaucomatous eyes show a great deal of overlap. An IOP cutoff value of 21 mm Hg thus has no real clinical significance. Several studies have indicated that as many as 50% of patients who have glaucomatous optic neuropathy and/or visual field loss have initial screening IOPs below 21 mm Hg. Furthermore, because of diurnal fluctuation, elevations of IOP may occur only intermittently in some glaucomatous eyes. Although elevated IOP is still considered a key feature of glaucoma, it is not considered essential to its diagnosis. Optic nerve head appearance and visual field defects have assumed predominant roles in the diagnosis of primary open-angle glaucoma.

Nonetheless, treatment is aimed at lowering the IOP. However, careful periodic evaluation of the optic disc and visual field is of great importance in the follow-up of glaucoma patients. Stereophotographic documentation or computerized imaging of the disc enhances the clinician's ability to detect change on follow-up. Pertinent clinical signs of glaucoma in the optic disc are asymmetry of the neuroretinal rim area, focal thinning of the neuroretinal rim, optic disc hemorrhage, and especially any acquired change in the disc rim appearance or the surrounding retinal nerve fiber layer. An attempt should be made to correlate changes in the optic disc with defects in the visual field.

Gonioscopy should be performed in all patients evaluated for glaucoma and repeated periodically in open-angle glaucoma patients to detect possible angle closure caused by miotic therapy or lens change. Repeat gonioscopy is also indicated when the chamber becomes shallow, when strong miotics are prescribed, after laser trabeculoplasty or iridotomy, and when IOP rises.

Associated Disorders

Myopia An association between primary open-angle glaucoma and myopia has been reported. It is possible that myopic individuals may be at increased risk for the development of glaucoma. Another possible explanation is that the association between myopia and primary open-angle glaucoma is influenced by selection bias, since persons who have refractive errors are more likely to seek eye care and thus have a higher probability than emmetropes of being diagnosed with glaucoma. The concurrence of these two conditions may complicate both diagnosis and management. Disc evaluation is particularly complicated in the presence of myopic fundus changes. Tilting of the disc may make an assessment of cupping difficult. Myopia-related retinal changes can cause visual field abnormalities apart from any glaucomatous process. High refractive error may also make it difficult to perform accurate perimetric measurement and to interpret visual field abnormalities. In addition, the magnification of the disc associated with the refractive error interferes with optic disc evaluation.

Diabetes mellitus Studies have reported a higher prevalence of both elevated mean IOP and of primary open-angle glaucoma among persons with diabetes compared to those without diabetes. In addition, glaucoma patients have been reported to have a higher prevalence of abnormal glucose metabolism than the general population. As with myopia it is unclear whether this association indicates that diabetes is a risk factor for glaucoma or whether it represents self-selection into the health care system. Some authorities believe that the small-vessel involvement in diabetes makes the optic disc more susceptible to pressure-related damage.

Cardiovascular disease Positive associations between blood pressure and IOP and between blood pressure and primary open-angle glaucoma have been reported. The hypothesis that systemic hypertension, with its possible microcirculatory effects on the optic disc, may lead to increased glaucoma susceptibility is biologically plausible. However, evidence that cardiovascular disease is a risk factor for glaucoma is weak. The possible role of arteriosclerotic and ischemic vascular disease is also unclear, but these factors may be important in the development of some cases of glaucoma, particularly those with IOP in the normal or low range.

Retinal vein occlusion Patients with central retinal vein occlusion (CRVO) often have elevated IOP or glaucoma in the affected eye and/or in the fellow eye. This relationship may be obscured by the temporary hypotony that often follows the vein occlusion. In susceptible individuals, eyes with elevated IOP are at risk of developing CRVO. Thus, elevated IOP in the fellow eye of an eye affected with retinal vein occlusion must be kept as low as reasonably possible.

Quigley HA. Nerve fiber layer assessment in managing glaucoma. In: *Focal Points: Clinical Modules for Ophthalmologists.* San Francisco: American Academy of Ophthalmology; 1988;6:5.

Schwartz B. Optic disc evaluation in glaucoma. In: *Focal Points: Clinical Modules for Ophthalmologists.* San Francisco: American Academy of Ophthalmology; 1990;8:12.

The Glaucoma Suspect

Elevated IOP or a suspicious-appearing optic disc or visual field can be reason to consider an individual a *glaucoma suspect.* The most common finding warranting this diagnosis is elevated IOP in the absence of identifiable optic nerve damage or visual field loss, a condition often termed ocular hypertension. Estimates of the prevalence of *ocular hypertension* vary considerably. Some authorities believe that the prevalence may be as high as 8 times that of definite primary open-angle glaucoma. Analysis of studies that have followed individuals with elevated IOP for variable time periods have indicated that the higher the baseline IOP, the greater the risk of developing glaucoma. However, it is important to note that even among individuals with elevated IOP, the vast majority never develop glaucoma.

It is often difficult to differentiate between a diagnosis of glaucoma suspect versus early primary open-angle glaucoma. The ophthalmologist must look carefully for signs of early damage to the optic nerve, such as focal notching, asymmetry of cupping, splinter disc hemorrhage, nerve fiber layer dropout, or subtle visual field defects. If these are present, a diagnosis of early primary open-angle glaucoma should be considered, and most ophthalmologists agree that treatment should be initiated.

No clear consensus exists on whether elevated IOP should be treated if no signs of early damage are present. Some ophthalmologists treat all individuals with elevated IOP, some do not treat without evidence of optic nerve damage, and some select and treat those individuals thought to be at greatest risk for developing glaucoma. This last approach is currently the most common.

All available data must be weighed in assessing the patient's risk for developing glaucoma and deciding whether or not to treat elevated IOP. The following risk factors should be considered:

- Level of elevated IOP
- Family history of glaucoma
- Race
- Age

Most ophthalmologists initiate treatment if the IOP is consistently higher than 30 mm Hg, because of the high risk of optic disc damage. If the clinician elects to treat solely on the basis of IOP, care must be taken that the risks of therapy do not exceed the risk of the disease. Furthermore, in patients without demonstrated damage to the optic nerve, the definition of IOP control can be less rigorous. For example, lowering the IOP of a patient with normal optic discs and visual fields from the 40s into the 20s might be satisfactory. Additional factors that may contribute to the decision to start ocular hypertensive therapy include the desires of the patient, reliability of visual fields, availability for follow-up visits, and ability to examine the optic disc.

The question of the effect of medical treatment compared to observation of individuals with elevated IOP but no signs of glaucoma is being addressed in an ongoing multicenter randomized clinical trial. This study should also help identify what characteristics or combinations of characteristics place these individuals at increased risk of developing optic nerve damage.

Quality of Care Committee, Glaucoma Panel. *The Glaucoma Suspect* (Preferred Practice Pattern). San Francisco: American Academy of Ophthalmology; 1995.

Normal- (Low-) Tension Glaucoma

Considerable controversy remains about whether normal-tension glaucoma represents a distinct disease entity or is simply primary open-angle glaucoma with IOP within the normal range. Because IOP is a continuous variable with no definite dividing line between normal and abnormal, many authorities are questioning whether the term *low-tension,* or *normal-tension, glaucoma* should be abandoned. This debate is likely to persist for years. Whatever the outcome, the concept of normal-tension glaucoma has undeniably had a strong influence on the classification and understanding of glaucoma.

Clinical Features

As previously emphasized, elevated IOP is an important risk factor in the development of glaucoma, but it is not the only risk factor. In normal-tension glaucoma other risk factors, most of which are currently unknown, may play a more important role than does IOP. Many authorities have hypothesized that local vascular factors may have an important role in the development of this disorder. Studies have suggested that patients with normal-tension glaucoma show a higher prevalence of vasospastic disorders such as migraine headache and Raynaud phenomenon, ischemic vascular diseases, autoimmune diseases, and coagulopathies compared to patients with high-tension glaucoma. However, these findings have not been consistent.

Field loss consistent with glaucoma has been noted after a decrease in blood pressure following a hypotensive crisis. However, damage that is secondary to such a specific precipitating event tends to be stable and does not progress once the underlying problem has been corrected. Most cases of normal-tension glaucoma are not caused by a sudden precipitating event. The condition is characteristically progressive, often despite the lowering of IOP. The association between IOP and normal-tension glaucoma and, accordingly, the efficacy of lowering IOP, is debatable. Studies have indicated that in glaucomatous eyes with normal but asymmetric IOPs, the worse damage usually occurs in the eye with the higher IOP. But, as this association does not hold for all eyes, other factors must be operative as well.

Another area of considerable debate concerns patterns of optic disc damage and visual field loss in normal-tension glaucoma compared to high-tension open-angle glaucoma. In eyes matched for total visual field loss, the neuroretinal rim has been reported to be thinner, especially inferiorly and inferotemporally, in those with normal-tension glaucoma. Varied patterns of peripapillary atrophy may also be more common. Some authorities have separated normal-tension glaucoma into two forms based on disc appearance: a *senile sclerotic group* with shallow, pale sloping of the neuroretinal rim (primarily in older patients with vascular disease); and a *focal ischemic group* with deep, focal, polar notching in the neuroretinal rim.

The visual field defects in normal-tension glaucoma have been described as more focal, deeper, and closer to fixation, especially early in the course of the disease, compared to what is commonly seen in high-tension glaucoma. A dense paracentral scotoma involving fixation is not an unusual finding as the initial defect. The validity of many of the reports of purported differences between normal-tension and high-tension open-angle glaucoma has been disputed by other studies that have found no differences in these characteristics.

Differential Diagnosis

Many conditions can mimic normal-tension glaucoma, including several that can cause arcuate-type visual field defects. These conditions are vascular occlusion, optic nerve head drusen, optic nerve head pits and colobomas, chorioretinitis, retinal detachment, retinoschisis, chiasmal tumors, and anterior ischemic optic neuropathy.

Care must be taken to distinguish normal-tension glaucoma from undetected high-tension glaucoma and nonglaucomatous optic nerve disease (Table VII-1). Repeated IOP measurements at different times of the day are necessary to ensure that glaucomatous damage is occurring with IOPs consistently in the normal range.

TABLE VII-1

Undetected high-tension glaucoma

Primary open-angle glaucoma with diurnal IOP variation

Intermittent IOP elevation
  Angle-closure glaucoma
  Glaucomatocyclitic crisis

Previously elevated IOP
  Old secondary glaucoma (e.g., steroid-induced glaucoma, uveitic glaucoma, etc.)
  Normalized IOP in an eye with previously elevated IOP

Use of medication that may cause IOP lowering

Tonometric error

Nonglaucomatous optic nerve disease

Congenital anomalies

Compressive lesions of optic nerve and chiasm

Shock optic neuropathy

Anterior ischemic optic neuropathy

Retinal disorders, i.e., retinal detachment, retinoschisis

Elevated IOPs can be obscured in patients taking systemic medication, particularly beta blockers, and by artifactually low tonometric readings. Other conditions to consider in the differential diagnosis include normalized IOP in an eye with previously elevated IOP, intermittent angle-closure glaucoma, and previous corticosteroid-induced or other secondary glaucoma.

Diagnostic Evaluation

It is difficult to know how often glaucomatous damage occurs with IOP in the normal range. Population-based epidemiological studies have suggested that as many as 30%–50% of glaucomatous eyes may have IOPs below 21 mm Hg on a single reading. Repeated testing would undoubtedly have detected elevated IOPs in many of these eyes. The prevalence of normal-tension glaucoma appears to vary among different populations. Studies have suggested that among Japanese patients, a particularly high proportion of open-angle glaucoma occurs with IOP in the normal range. Among clinic-based patients, a diagnosis of normal-tension glaucoma is influenced by how thoroughly other possible causes of optic neuropathy are considered and eliminated.

Before making a diagnosis of normal-tension glaucoma, the clinician should measure the IOP by applanation tonometry. Diurnal pressure readings should be considered. Gonioscopy should be performed to rule out angle closure, angle recession, or evidence of previous intraocular inflammation. Careful stereoscopic disc evaluation is essential to rule out other congenital or acquired disc anomalies. The clinician must also consider the patient's medical history, particularly any history of cardiovascular disease and low blood pressure caused by hemorrhage, myocardial infarction, or shock.

Sometimes a diagnosis cannot be established on the basis of ophthalmic examination, particularly if findings are atypical, as in unilateral disease, decreased central vision, or visual field loss not consistent with the optic disc appearance. In such cases medical and neurological evaluation should be considered, including tests for anemia, heart disease, syphilis, and temporal arteritis or other causes of systemic vasculitis. Auscultation and palpation of the carotid arteries should be performed. Ophthalmodynamometry and other noninvasive tests of carotid circulation are helpful in some cases. Increasing attention is being focused on assessment of ocular blood flow, but techniques for these measurements are generally still investigational. Evaluation of the optic nerve in the chiasmal region with CT scans or MRI may be warranted in some cases to rule out compressive lesions.

Prognosis and Therapy

The therapy for normal-tension glaucoma is difficult and controversial. Therapy is generally instituted for normal-tension glaucoma unless it is determined that the optic neuropathy is stable, as is often the case in patients with a history of shock. A prospective collaborative trial of treatment versus no treatment is under way, and it may provide treatment standards in the future. While proof of efficacy may be lacking, the goal of therapy should be to achieve an IOP as low as possible without inducing complications.

As with primary open-angle glaucoma, medical therapy is the most common initial approach in treating normal-tension glaucoma. As with all glaucomas, it is useful for the ophthalmologist to change or add medications to one eye at a time, so that the contralateral eye can be used as a control to assess therapeutic response. If medications are inadequate, laser trabeculoplasty is sometimes effective in reducing IOP. Glaucoma filtering surgery, possibly combined with an antifibrotic agent, may be indicated, as this procedure tends to produce the lowest IOP. Unfortunately, some patients continue to lose visual field despite concerted efforts to lower IOP.

Systemic medications such as calcium channel blockers are advocated by some authorities because of the possible beneficial effects of increasing capillary perfusion of the optic nerve head. The efficacy of this treatment, however, has not yet been definitely demonstrated. If systemic treatment with calcium channel blockers is undertaken, it should be coordinated with the patient's primary care physician because of possible side effects.

Jampel HD. Normal (low) tension glaucoma. In: *Focal Points: Clinical Modules for Ophthalmologists.* San Francisco: American Academy of Ophthalmology; 1991;9:12.

Secondary Open-Angle Glaucoma

Exfoliation Syndrome (Pseudoexfoliation)

Exfoliation syndrome is characterized by the deposition of a distinctive fibrillar material in the anterior segment of the eye. Histologically, this material has been found in and on the lens epithelium and capsule, pupillary margin, ciliary epithelium, iris pigment epithelium, iris stroma and blood vessels, and subconjunctival tissue. Although its origin is not known precisely, it probably arises from multiple sources as part of a generalized basement membrane disorder. Histochemically, the material resembles amyloid.

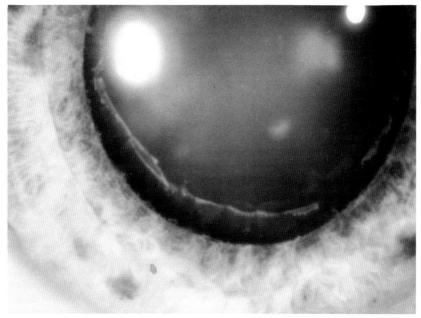

FIG VII-1—Evidence of exfoliative material deposited on the anterior lens capsule. Exfoliative material may also be deposited on other structures within the anterior segment, including the iris, ciliary processes, peripheral retina, and the conjunctiva.

Deposits occur in a targetlike pattern on the anterior lens capsule and are best seen after pupil dilation. A central area and a peripheral zone of deposition are usually separated by an intermediate clear area, where iris movement presumably rubs the material from the lens (Fig VII-1). The material is sometimes visible on the iris at the edge of the pupil. Deposits also occur on the zonular fibers of the lens, ciliary processes, anterior chamber angle, and corneal endothelium. In aphakic individuals, these deposits are seen on the anterior hyaloid as well. The chamber angle often has abnormally irregular, heavy trabecular pigment as well as pigment deposited anterior to Schwalbe's line (Sampaolesi's line). The chamber angle is often shallow, presumably as a result of anterior movement of the lens–iris diaphragm related to zonular weakness.

In addition to the typical deposits and pigmentation, other anterior segment abnormalities are also noted. Fine pigment deposits often appear on the iris surface, and peripupillary atrophy with transillumination of the pupillary margin is common. A more scattered, diffuse depigmentation may also occur, with transillumination defect over the entire sphincter region. Phacodonesis and iridodonesis are not uncommon, and they are most likely related to zonular weakness, which may predispose these affected eyes to zonular dehiscence, vitreous loss, and other complications during cataract surgery. Iris angiography has demonstrated abnormalities of the iris vessels through fluorescein leakage.

Exfoliation syndrome may be monocular or binocular with varying degrees of asymmetry. The apparently uninvolved fellow eye may develop the syndrome at a later time. Exfoliation syndrome is associated with open-angle glaucoma in all populations, although the prevalence varies considerably. In Scandinavian countries exfoliation syndrome accounts for more than 50% of cases of open-angle glaucoma. This syndrome is strongly age-related: it is rarely seen under the age of 50 and occurs most commonly in individuals over the age of 70.

The open-angle glaucoma associated with exfoliation syndrome is thought to be caused by the fibrillar material obstructing flow through the trabecular meshwork. Exfoliation syndrome with glaucoma differs somewhat from primary open-angle glaucoma. It is often monocular and shows greater pigmentation of the trabecular meshwork. Furthermore, the IOP is often higher than it is in primary open-angle glaucoma, and the overall prognosis is worse, as the condition often seems more resistant to medical therapy. Lens extraction does not alleviate the condition. Laser trabeculoplasty can be very effective in this condition, but the response may not be long lasting. Trabeculectomy is often associated with good results.

Pigmentary Glaucoma

The *pigment dispersion syndrome* consists of pigment deposition on the corneal endothelium in a vertical spindle pattern (Krukenberg spindle), in the trabecular meshwork, and on the lens periphery. The spindle pattern on the posterior cornea is caused by the aqueous convection currents and subsequent phagocytosis of pigment by the corneal endothelium. Characteristic spokelike loss of the iris pigment epithelium occurs; it is manifested as transillumination defects in the iris midperiphery (Fig VII-2). The peripheral iris transillumination defects appear in front of the lens

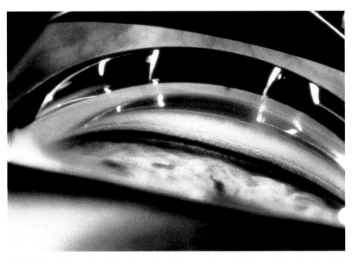

FIG VII-2—Characteristic heavy, uniform pigmentation of the trabecular meshwork seen in the pigment dispersion syndrome and pigmentary glaucoma.

zonular fibers, suggesting that mechanical contact between the zonular packets and the iris contributes to the iris pigment release. Some authorities believe that the presence of Krukenberg spindles is not absolutely necessary to make the diagnosis of pigment dispersion syndrome.

This syndrome may or may not be associated with glaucoma. An individual with pigment dispersion syndrome may or may not ever develop elevated IOP. Various studies have suggested that the risk of an individual with this syndrome developing glaucoma is approximately 25%–50%. Pigmentary glaucoma occurs most commonly in myopic males between the ages of 20 and 50 years. Affected females tend to be older than affected males.

Pigmentary glaucoma is characterized by wide fluctuations in IOP. High IOP often occurs when pigment is released into the aqueous humor, such as following exercise or pupillary dilation. Symptoms may include halos and intermittent visual blurring. With age the signs and symptoms of pigmentary dispersion may decrease in some individuals, possibly as a result of normal growth of the lens and an increase in physiological pupillary block. Loss of accommodation may also be a factor.

Medical treatment is often successful in reducing IOP, but young patients tolerate miotic therapy poorly. They respond reasonably well to laser trabeculoplasty, although the effect may be short-lived. Filtering surgery is usually successful.

Posterior bowing of the iris with reverse pupillary block configuration is noted in many eyes that have pigmentary glaucoma. This iris configuration may result in greater contact of the zonular fibers with the posterior iris surface with a subsequent increase of pigment release. Laser iridotomy has been proposed as a means of minimizing posterior bowing of the iris (Fig VII-3). However, the effectiveness of laser iridotomy for the treatment of pigmentary glaucoma has not been definitively established.

Liebmann JM. Pigmentary glaucoma: new insights. In: *Focal Points: Clinical Modules for Ophthalmologists.* San Francisco: American Academy of Ophthalmology; 1998;16:2.

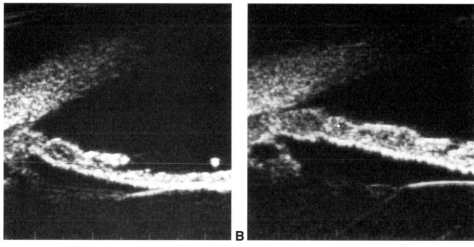

A **B**

FIG VII-3—*A,* Ultrasound biomicroscopy image of concave iris configuration in pigmentary glaucoma, pre–laser treatment. *B,* Same eye, post–laser treatment. (Photographs courtesy of Charles J. Pavlin, MD.)

Lens-Induced Glaucoma

Lens-induced open-angle glaucoma occurs in three clinical forms: phacolytic glaucoma, lens particle glaucoma, and phacoanaphylaxis. (See also BCSC Section 4, *Ophthalmic Pathology and Intraocular Tumors,* and BCSC Section 9, *Intraocular Inflammation and Uveitis.*)

Phacolytic glaucoma occurs as a result of the leakage of lens proteins from a mature or hypermature cataract. This leakage is often accompanied by pain and marked anterior chamber inflammation. The trabecular meshwork becomes blocked by macrophages and high-molecular-weight lens proteins. While medications to control the IOP should be used immediately, definitive therapy requires cataract extraction.

Lens particle glaucoma may occur after acute penetrating lens injury or after extracapsular cataract extraction with retained lens material. Cortical material and associated inflammatory cells cause obstruction of the outflow pathways. If possible, medical therapy should be initiated to control the IOP while the residual lens material resorbs. Appropriate therapy includes medications to decrease aqueous formation, mydriatics to inhibit posterior synechiae formation, and topical corticosteroids to reduce inflammation. If the glaucoma cannot be controlled, surgical removal of the lens material is necessary.

Phacoanaphylaxis is a condition that occurs after penetrating trauma or surgery. Patients become sensitized to their own lens proteins and develop a granulomatous reaction around the lens. If the inflammation involves the trabecular meshwork, these patients develop glaucoma. Phacoanaphylaxis is treated medically with corticosteroids and aqueous suppressants to reduce inflammation and IOP. If medical treatment is unsuccessful, residual lens material should be removed.

Intraocular Tumors

Intraocular tumors may produce secondary glaucoma by a variety of mechanisms, including direct tumor invasion of the anterior chamber angle; angle closure by rotation of the ciliary body or anterior displacement of the lens–iris diaphragm; intraocular hemorrhage; neovascularization of the angle; and deposition of tumor cells, inflammatory cells, and cellular debris within the trabecular meshwork. In adults, tumors causing glaucoma include uveal melanoma, metastatic carcinoma, lymphomas, and leukemia. In children, glaucoma is associated with retinoblastoma, juvenile xanthogranuloma, and medulloepithelioma.

Ocular Inflammation and Secondary Open-Angle Glaucoma

Secondary open-angle glaucoma can result from *ocular inflammatory diseases* such as acute iridocyclitis, episcleritis, scleritis, keratitis, and posterior uveitis. Usually, acute iridocyclitis is associated with low IOP from decreased aqueous humor formation and increased uveoscleral flow. Sometimes aqueous outflow is obstructed by clogging of the trabecular meshwork by white blood cells or particulate debris, swelling of the endothelial cells lining the trabecular columns, or increased viscosity of the aqueous humor.

The presence of keratic precipitates and a miotic pupil suggests *iritis* as the cause of the IOP elevation. Gonioscopic evaluation may reveal subtle trabecular meshwork precipitates. Sometimes, peripheral anterior synechiae or posterior synechiae with iris bombé may develop, resulting in angle closure. The treatment of inflammatory glaucoma is complicated by the fact that corticosteroid treatment may raise IOP, either by reducing inflammation and improving aqueous production or by obstructing outflow. Miotic agents should be avoided in patients with iritis, because they may aggravate the inflammation and cause posterior synechiae.

Glaucoma may occur with *viral inflammations* of the eye, including herpes simplex, herpes zoster, rubella, and mumps.

Glaucomatocyclitic crisis (Posner-Schlossman syndrome) is a condition in which recurrent attacks of acute IOP elevation are associated with minimal signs of intraocular inflammation. The IOP elevations may be high enough to cause corneal edema. The attacks usually subside spontaneously in a few days; they are usually unilateral but occasionally bilateral. Prostaglandins have been implicated in the pathogenesis of this condition. Although optic nerve damage rarely occurs during acute attacks of glaucomatocyclitic crisis, some patients eventually develop visual field loss, and some seem to develop chronic open-angle glaucoma. Patients with this condition can often tell when an attack is beginning and begin self-therapy with aqueous suppressants and/or topical corticosteroids.

Fuchs heterochromic iridocyclitis is a syndrome that includes heterochromia (asymmetry of iris color), cataract, and low-grade iritis. The condition is most often unilateral. The iritis is mild and does not cause posterior synechiae or peripheral anterior synechiae. The heterochromia is characterized by loss of stromal pigment in the involved eye. Thus, the lighter-colored iris usually indicates the involved eye. However, in blue-eyed individuals, the affected eye may become darker as the stromal atrophy progresses and the darker iris pigmented epithelium shows through. Other findings include fine vitreous opacities and keratic precipitates that have a characteristic stellate appearance and are diffusely distributed on the posterior cornea. Very fine new vessels may be present in the anterior chamber angle, but they do not lead to synechial closure. The glaucoma may be difficult to control and does not correspond to the degree of inflammation. Corticosteroids are generally not effective in treating this condition. Aqueous suppressants are the agents of choice.

Raised Episcleral Venous Pressure

A variety of conditions that raise episcleral venous pressure also raise IOP. These conditions include retrobulbar tumors, thyroid ophthalmopathy, superior vena cava syndrome, carotid and dural fistulas, orbital varices, and Sturge-Weber syndrome. Dilated episcleral vessels are a prominent feature of Sturge-Weber syndrome. An idiopathic form of this disease, which may be familial, has been described.

In these situations medications that reduce aqueous humor formation are more effective than drugs that increase aqueous outflow. Laser trabeculoplasty is not effective unless there are secondary changes in the outflow channels. Glaucoma filtering surgery may be complicated by ciliochoroidal effusions or suprachoroidal hemorrhage.

Accidental and Surgical Trauma

Blunt or penetrating trauma may produce acute glaucoma as a result of direct injury to the trabecular meshwork or its obstruction by blood or inflammatory debris. Secondary open-angle glaucoma can also appear many years after blunt trauma. It is important to search carefully for signs of angle recession in any patient who presents with unilateral open-angle glaucoma.

Open-angle glaucoma is one of the long-term sequelae of siderosis or chalcosis from a retained intraocular metallic foreign body. Chemical injuries, particularly alkali, may cause acute secondary glaucoma as a result of inflammation, shrinkage of scleral collagen, release of chemical mediators such as prostaglandins, direct damage to the chamber angle, or compromise of the anterior uveal circulation. Trabecular damage or inflammation may cause glaucoma to develop months or years after a chemical injury.

Blunt trauma of the anterior segment may lead to *angle recession*. Histopathologically, angle recession is characterized by a tear through the ciliary body, most commonly between the longitudinal and circular muscle layers. Gonioscopically, angle recession is seen as an irregular widening of the ciliary body band and an absence of ciliary processes. The cause of outflow obstruction may be either direct damage to the trabecular meshwork or extension of an endothelial layer and subsequent Descemet's membrane from the cornea over the iridocorneal angle. In addition, a significant proportion (up to 50%) of fellow eyes may develop increased IOP, suggesting that perhaps many of the eyes with angle-recession glaucoma may have been predisposed to open-angle glaucoma.

The greater the extent of the angle recession, the greater the risk of glaucoma. Even with substantial angle recession, the risk of glaucoma is not high. Nonetheless, because it is not possible to predict which eyes will develop glaucoma, all eyes with angle recession must be followed closely for several years. The risk of developing glaucoma decreases appreciably after several years, and these eyes should continue to be examined annually. The treatment of angle-recession glaucoma is best accomplished with aqueous suppressants. Miotics may be useful, but paradoxical responses may occur. Laser trabeculoplasty has a poor chance of success but may be considered prior to filtering surgery.

Glaucoma may also result from closure of a *cyclodialysis cleft*. In contrast to angle recession, histopathologic examination of a cyclodialysis cleft shows a focal area of separation of the ciliary body from its attachment to the scleral spur. When a cyclodialysis cleft is present, the eye is often hypotonous. The mechanism of the hypotony is thought to be related to increased uveoscleral outflow, reduced aqueous production, or both. If the cleft closes, the IOP may become quite elevated. The trabecular meshwork function may improve spontaneously with time, requiring only temporary treatment of the IOP. Occasionally, long-term elevation of IOP persists, and this condition is treated in a manner similar to primary open-angle glaucoma.

Glaucoma may result from blunt trauma and *hyphema* but is more common following recurrent hemorrhage or rebleeding. The reported frequency of rebleeding following hyphema varies considerably in the literature, with an average incidence of 5%–10%. Rebleeding usually occurs within 5–7 days after the initial hyphema and may be related to normal clot retraction and lysis. In most cases the size of the hyphema associated with rebleeding is greater than the primary hyphema. In general, the larger the hyphema, the higher the incidence of glaucoma, although small hemorrhages may be associated with marked elevation of IOP and vice versa. Increased IOP is a result of obstruction of the trabecular meshwork with red blood cells, combined with other inflammatory cells, debris, plasma, and other direct effects of blunt trauma on the trabecular meshwork.

Individuals with *sickle cell hemoglobinopathies* have an increased incidence of glaucoma following hyphema. Normal red blood cells generally pass through the trabecular meshwork without difficulty. However, in the sickle cell hemoglobinopathies (including sickle trait), the red blood cells tend to sickle in the aqueous humor, and these more rigid cells have great difficulty passing out of the eye. In the sickle cell hemoglobinopathies, therefore, small amounts of blood in the anterior chamber may result in marked elevations of IOP. In addition, the optic discs of patients with sickle cell disease are much more sensitive to elevated IOP and are easily damaged, possibly as a result of compromised microvascular perfusion.

In general, an uncomplicated hyphema should be managed conservatively. Topical and systemic corticosteroids may reduce associated inflammation, although their effect on rebleeding is debatable. If there is significant ciliary spasm or photophobia, cycloplegic agents may be helpful, but they have no proven benefit in terms of rebleeding. Aminocaproic acid has been shown to reduce rebleeding, but reports on its efficacy and associated complications are conflicting. Patching and bed rest are also advocated by some authors, although these precautions are of unproven value. If the IOP is elevated, aqueous suppressants and hyperosmotic agents are recommended. It has been suggested that patients with sickle cell hemoglobinopathies should avoid carbonic anhydrase inhibitors, as they may increase the sickling tendency in the anterior chamber by increasing aqueous levels of ascorbic acid; however, this relationship has not been firmly established. Adrenergic agonists and parasympathomimetic agents should be avoided.

Persistently elevated IOP may require treatment with surgery. In the management of young children, an additional consideration that may justify early surgical intervention is the potential of inducing amblyopia if the hyphema is significantly obstructing vision. If surgery for increased IOP becomes necessary, an anterior chamber irrigation or washout procedure is commonly tried first. If a total hyphema is present, pupillary block may occur. An iridectomy is helpful in such cases. If the IOP remains uncontrolled, a trabeculectomy may be required. Some surgeons prefer to perform a trabeculectomy as the initial surgical procedure to obtain immediate IOP control, with the understanding that the trabeculectomy will most likely eventually fail.

Hemolytic and/or ghost cell glaucoma may develop after vitreous hemorrhage. In *hemolytic glaucoma* hemoglobin-laden macrophages block the trabecular outflow channels. Red-tinged cells are seen floating in the anterior chamber, and a reddish brown discoloration of the trabecular meshwork is often present. In *ghost cell glaucoma* rigid degenerated red blood cells (erythroclasts) block the aqueous outflow channels. These khaki-colored ghost cells may be observed floating in the anterior chamber or visualized gonioscopically in the trabecular meshwork. Sometimes the ghost cells may appear as a pseudohypopyon in the inferior chamber angle. Both hemolytic and ghost cell glaucoma are generally self-limiting and resolve once the hemorrhage has cleared. Thus, medical therapy with aqueous suppressants is the preferred initial approach. However, if medical therapy fails to control marked elevations of IOP, some patients may require irrigation of the anterior chamber with flow directed toward the angle recess. If washout is ineffective, or if IOP increases again with recurrence of ghost cells, vitrectomy may be needed.

Operative procedures such as cataract extraction, filtering surgery, or corneal transplantation may be followed by an increase in IOP. Similarly, laser surgery, including trabeculoplasty, iridotomy, and posterior capsulotomy, may be complicated by posttreatment IOP elevation. The IOP may rise as high as 50 mm Hg or more; these elevations are usually transient, lasting from a few hours to a few days. The mechanism is not known, but pigment release, inflammatory debris, and mechanical deformation of the trabecular meshwork have all been implicated.

In addition, agents used as adjuncts to intraocular surgery may cause secondary IOP elevations. For example, injection of viscoelastic substances such as sodium hyaluronate into the anterior chamber may result in a transient and possibly severe postoperative increase in IOP.

Such postoperative pressure elevation can cause considerable damage to the optic nerve of a susceptible individual. Eyes with preexisting glaucoma are at particular risk for further damage. Elevated IOP may also increase the risk of a retinal vascular occlusion. Thus, it is important to measure IOP soon after surgery or laser treatment. If a substantial rise in IOP does occur, ocular hypertensive therapy may be required. Usually, use of beta-adrenergic antagonists, alpha$_2$-adrenergic agonists, or carbonic anhydrase inhibitors is adequate. However, hyperosmotic agents are sometimes necessary.

Drugs and Glaucoma

Application of topical corticosteroids to the eye can sometimes raise IOP, depending on corticosteroid strength and on frequency and duration of administration. The extent of the IOP elevation may range from mild to severe. A high percentage of patients with primary open-angle glaucoma demonstrate this IOP response to topical corticosteroids. Systemic administration of corticosteroids may also raise IOP in some individuals, although less frequently than topical administration. A corticosteroid-induced rise in pressure may cause glaucomatous optic nerve damage in some patients. This condition can mimic primary open-angle glaucoma in the adult or infantile glaucoma in the child. Usually, discontinuing the corticosteroid allows the IOP to return to pretreatment levels. Corticosteroid-induced glaucoma may develop at any time during long-term corticosteroid administration. IOP thus needs to be monitored in such patients. Some corticosteroid preparations (e.g., fluorometholone or medrysone) are less likely to raise IOP than are prednisolone or dexamethasone. However, even weaker corticosteroids or lower concentrations of stronger drugs can raise IOP in susceptible individuals.

Patients with excessive levels of endogenous corticosteroids (e.g., Cushing syndrome) can also develop increased IOP. Generally, IOP returns to normal when the corticosteroid-producing tumor or hyperplastic tissue is excised.

Cycloplegic drugs can increase IOP in individuals with open angles. Patients with primary open-angle glaucoma are more susceptible.

Epstein DL. *Chandler and Grant's Glaucoma*. 3rd ed. Philadelphia: Lea & Febiger; 1986.

Ritch R, Shields MB, Krupin T, eds. *The Glaucomas*. St Louis: CV Mosby Co; 1996.

Shields MB. *Textbook of Glaucoma*. 3rd ed. Baltimore: Williams & Wilkins; 1992.

CHAPTER VIII

Angle-Closure Glaucoma

Mechanisms and Pathophysiology of Angle Closure

Angle-closure glaucoma develops because apposition of the iris to the trabecular meshwork blocks the drainage of aqueous humor. Conceptually, the mechanisms of angle-closure glaucoma fall into two general categories: those that push the iris forward from behind and those that pull it forward into contact with the trabecular meshwork (Table VIII-1).

TABLE VIII-1

MECHANISMS OF ANGLE CLOSURE

IRIS PUSHED FORWARD	IRIS PULLED FORWARD
Pupillary block	Rubeosis iridis
Plateau iris	Inflammation
Tumors	Iridocorneal endothelial syndrome
Choroidal hemorrhage or effusion	

Pupillary block, with forward bowing of the iris, is the most frequent cause of angle-closure glaucoma. The flow of aqueous from the posterior chamber through the pupil is impeded, and this obstruction causes aqueous to build up behind the iris. The trapped aqueous forces the iris to bow forward against the trabecular meshwork (Fig VIII-1). This sequence is the mechanism for primary pupillary block associated with acute, subacute, and chronic angle-closure glaucoma.

Angle-closure glaucoma may also occur without pupillary block. The lens–iris diaphragm can be pushed forward by a tumor or other space-occupying lesion. In addition, the lens–iris diaphragm may come forward when the ciliary body swells and rotates about its insertion into the scleral spur. Conditions associated with the mechanism of a mass posterior to the lens–iris diaphragm pushing anteriorly include the following:

☐ Central retinal vein occlusion

☐ Ciliary body swelling, inflammation, or cysts

☐ Ciliary-block (malignant) glaucoma

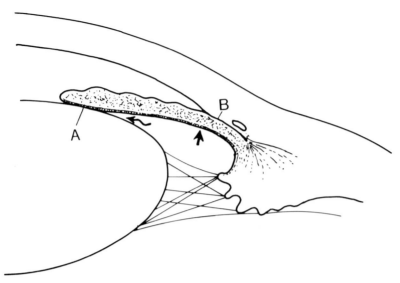

FIG VIII-1—Pupillary-block glaucoma. A functional block between the lens and iris *(A)* leads to increased pressure in the posterior chamber (arrows) with forward shift of the peripheral iris and closure of the anterior chamber angle *(B)*. (Reproduced with permission from Shields MB. *Textbook of Glaucoma.* 3rd ed. Baltimore: Williams & Wilkins; 1992.)

- Posterior segment tumors
- Contracting retrolental tissue
- Scleral buckling procedures
- Panretinal photocoagulation
- Nanophthalmos

Finally, the iris may also adhere to the trabecular meshwork following inflammation, neovascularization, or endothelial proliferation.

Primary Angle-Closure Glaucoma with Pupillary Block

Epidemiology

Heredity influences the development of primary angle-closure glaucoma with pupillary block. However, even though the potential for primary angle-closure glaucoma is probably inherited, family history is not useful in predicting a future angle-closure attack. The disease is considerably less common than primary open-angle glaucoma. The prevalence of primary angle-closure glaucoma increases with age as the depth and volume of the anterior chamber angle decrease.

Acute primary angle-closure glaucoma is unusual in the black population. Angle-closure glaucoma that occurs in black patients is usually chronic. Angle-closure glaucoma is less common among American Indians than whites, although it is more common among Canadian, Alaskan, and Greenland Inuit. Asians show a higher incidence of chronic angle-closure glaucoma, which is probably the major type of glaucoma in China (70% of glaucoma cases). Prevalence of primary angle-closure glaucoma is higher in women than in men. Hyperopic eyes have smaller anterior chambers and are at greater risk for developing angle-closure glaucoma.

Pathophysiology

Patients who develop primary angle-closure glaucoma tend to have small anterior segments, predisposing them to increased relative pupillary block. Relative pupillary block increases with age as the lens grows and the pupil becomes miotic. An angle-closure attack is often precipitated by some minor event, such as pupillary dilation. The dilation to midposition relaxes the peripheral iris so that it may bow forward into contact with the trabecular meshwork; in this position lens–iris apposition is maximal, setting the stage for pupillary block.

Acute Primary Angle-Closure Glaucoma

Acute primary angle-closure glaucoma is a condition that occurs when IOP rises rapidly as a result of relatively sudden blockage of the trabecular meshwork by the iris. It may be manifested by pain, blurred vision, rainbow-colored halos around lights, nausea, and vomiting. The rise in IOP to relatively high levels causes corneal epithelial edema, which is responsible for the visual symptoms.

Signs of acute angle-closure glaucoma include

- High IOP
- Middilated, sluggish, and often irregular pupil
- Corneal epithelial edema
- Congested episcleral and conjunctival blood vessels
- Shallow anterior chamber
- A mild amount of aqueous flare and cells

The optic nerve may be swollen during an acute attack.

Definitive diagnosis depends on the gonioscopic verification of angle closure. Gonioscopy should be possible in almost all acute angle-closure attacks, although medical treatment of elevated IOP and clearing of corneal edema with topical glycerin may be necessary to enable visualization of the chamber angle. Compression gonioscopy may help the physician to determine if the iris–trabecular meshwork blockage is reversible (appositional closure) or irreversible (synechial closure), and it may be therapeutic in breaking the attack of acute angle-closure glaucoma. Since primary angle-closure glaucoma is a bilateral disease, gonioscopy of the fellow eye usually reveals a narrow, occludable angle.

During an acute attack, IOP may be high enough to cause glaucomatous optic nerve damage and/or retinal vascular occlusion. Peripheral anterior synechiae (PAS) may form rapidly, and IOP-induced ischemia may produce sector atrophy of the iris. Such atrophy releases pigment and causes pigmentary dusting of the iris surface and corneal endothelium. Because of iris ischemia, the pupil may be permanently fixed and dilated. *Glaukomflecken,* characteristic small anterior subcapsular lens opacities, may also develop. These findings are helpful in detecting previous episodes of acute angle-closure glaucoma.

The definitive treatment for acute angle closure is either laser iridotomy or surgical iridectomy, which are discussed in detail in chapter XII. Mild attacks may be broken by cholinergic agents (pilocarpine 1%–2%), which induce miosis that pulls the peripheral iris away from the trabecular meshwork. However, when the IOP is quite elevated (e.g., above 40–50 mm Hg), the pupillary sphincter may be ischemic and unresponsive to miotic agents alone. The patient should be treated with some combination of a topical beta-adrenergic antagonist; alpha$_2$-adrenergic agonists; an oral, topical, or intravenous carbonic anhydrase inhibitor; and a hyperosmotic agent. This treatment is used to reduce IOP to the point where the miotic agent will constrict the pupil and open the angle. Peribulbar anesthesia, globe compression, and surgical paracentesis have also been described to treat acute angle-closure glaucoma.

The fellow eye, which shares the anatomic predisposition for increased pupillary block, is at high risk for developing acute angle-closure glaucoma. In addition, the pain and emotional upset resulting from the involvement of the first eye may increase sympathetic flow to the fellow eye and produce pupillary dilation.

In general, primary angle-closure glaucoma is a bilateral disease. Its occurrence in a patient whose fellow eye has a deep chamber angle raises the possibility of a secondary cause, such as a posterior segment mass. An untreated fellow eye has a 40%–80% chance of developing an acute attack of angle-closure glaucoma over the next 5–10 years. Long-term pilocarpine administration is not effective in preventing acute attacks in many cases, and it may even prevent the detection of chronic angle-closure glaucoma by decreasing the IOP. Thus, prophylactic iridectomy should be performed in the contralateral eye unless the angle clearly appears to be non-occludable.

Laser iridotomy is the treatment of choice for angle-closure glaucoma. Surgical iridectomy is indicated when laser iridotomy cannot be accomplished. Once an iridotomy has been performed, pupillary block is relieved and the iris is no longer pushed forward into contact with the trabecular meshwork. If a laser iridotomy cannot be performed, the acute attack can also be stopped by flattening the peripheral iris through gonioplasty or iridoplasty or by peaking the pupil with a laser. Following resolution of the acute attack, it is important to reevaluate the angle by gonioscopy for residual angle closure that may be amenable to laser gonioplasty. (See chapter XII for detailed discussion of these procedures.)

Subacute Angle-Closure Glaucoma

Subacute (intermittent or prodromal) angle-closure glaucoma is a condition characterized by episodes of blurred vision, halos, and mild pain caused by elevated IOP. These symptoms resolve spontaneously, especially during sleep, and IOP is usually normal between the episodes, which occur periodically over days or weeks. These episodes may be confused with headaches or migraines. The correct diagnosis can only be made with a high index of suspicion and gonioscopy. The typical history and the gonioscopic appearance of a narrow chamber angle help establish the diagnosis. Laser iridotomy is the treatment of choice in subacute angle-closure glaucoma. This condition can progress to acute or chronic angle-closure glaucoma.

Chronic Angle-Closure Glaucoma

Chronic angle-closure glaucoma is a condition that may develop either after acute angle-closure glaucoma or when the chamber angle closes gradually and IOP rises slowly. Permanent peripheral anterior synechiae may or may not be present; indentation gonioscopy can be used to make this determination. The clinical course resembles that of open-angle glaucoma in its lack of symptoms, modest elevation of IOP, progressive cupping of the optic nerve head, and characteristic glaucomatous loss of visual field. The diagnosis of chronic angle-closure glaucoma is frequently overlooked, and it is commonly confused with chronic open-angle glaucoma. Gonioscopic examination is important to enable the ophthalmologist to make the correct diagnosis.

Even if miotics and other agents lower IOP, iridotomy is necessary to relieve the pupillary block. Without iridotomy, closure of the angle progresses and becomes irreversible. For most chronic angle-closure glaucoma patients, iridotomy with or without chronic use of ocular hypotensive medication will control the disease; for others, subsequent filtering surgery or laser trabeculoplasty to the remaining open angle will be required. No clinical test can reliably determine whether or not an iridotomy alone will control the disease for an individual patient. However, since laser iridotomy is a relatively low-risk procedure compared to other surgical procedures, it should be performed before a more invasive or risky operative procedure. Individuals with extensive PAS and elevated IOP following acute angle closure may be helped by argon laser gonioplasty or goniosynechialysis.

Provocative Tests for Angle Closure

Only a small percentage of patients with shallow anterior chambers develop angle-closure glaucoma. Many clinicians have attempted to predict which asymptomatic patients with normal IOP will develop angle closure by performing a variety of provocative tests. These tests are designed to precipitate a limited form of angle closure, which can then be detected by gonioscopy and IOP measurement. The tests commonly used include darkroom, prone position, pharmacologic pupillary dilation, and prone-darkroom. An IOP increase of 8 mm Hg or more is considered positive. An asymmetric pressure rise between the two eyes with a corresponding degree of angle closure is also considered a positive sign. However, none of the provocative tests has been verified in a prospective study, and the predictive value of any provocative test has never been demonstrated. Ultimately, the decision to treat an asymptomatic patient with narrow angles rests on the clinical judgment of the ophthalmologist.

Any patient with narrow angles, regardless of the results of provocative testing, should be advised of the symptoms of angle-closure glaucoma, of the need for immediate ophthalmic attention if symptoms occur, and of the value of long-term periodic follow-up.

Various factors that cause pupillary dilation may induce angle-closure glaucoma. These factors include a variety of drugs as well as pain, emotional upset, or fright. In predisposed eyes with shallow anterior chambers, either mydriatic or miotic agents can precipitate angle-closure glaucoma. Mydriatic agents include not only dilating drops but also systemic medications that cause dilation. The effect of miotics is to pull the peripheral iris movement away from the chamber angle. However, miotics also cause the zonular fibers of the lens to relax, allowing the lens to come forward. Furthermore, their use results in an increase in the amount of iris–lens contact, thus increasing pupillary block. For these reasons, miotics, especially the cholinesterase inhibitors, may also induce or aggravate angle-closure glaucoma. Gonioscopy should be repeated soon after miotic drugs are administered to patients with narrow angles.

A number of systemic medications, including some nonprescription preparations, carry warnings against use by patients with glaucoma. Most of these drugs have the potential for precipitating angle-closure glaucoma in susceptible individuals because of anticholinergic or sympathomimetic activity. While systemic administration generally does not raise intraocular drug levels to the same degree as does topical administration, even slight mydriasis in a patient with a critically narrow chamber angle can induce angle-closure glaucoma. Patients with narrow angles who have not had an iridotomy or iridectomy should be warned about this possibility.

The use of an alpha-adrenergic blocker has been suggested to reverse the effects of sympathomimetic dilating agents and minimize the chances of angle closure. Moxisylyte (thymoxamine), which is not commercially available, and dapiprazole, available in a 0.5% solution, both reverse phenylephrine- or tropicamide-induced pupillary dilation to baseline within 30 minutes compared to 3 hours when no alpha-adrenergic blocker is used. However, this suggested combination of alpha-adrenergic agonist and adrenergic antagonist does not eliminate the possibility of precipitating angle-closure glaucoma; it just gets the eye through the critical mid-dilation stage more quickly. Moxisylyte has also been used as a diagnostic test for combined-mechanism glaucoma. Because it produces miosis without affecting the ciliary body–controlled facility of outflow, it can sometimes open a narrow or appositionally closed angle and separate the angle-closure component from the open-angle component in combined-mechanism glaucoma.

Primary Angle-Closure Glaucoma Without Pupillary Block

Plateau iris is an unusual type of angle-closure glaucoma caused by anteriorly positioned ciliary processes that critically narrow the anterior chamber recess. There is often a component of pupillary block. Following dilation of the pupil, the peripheral iris bunches up and obstructs the trabecular meshwork (Fig VIII-2). Plateau iris may be suspected if the central anterior chamber seems unusually deep and the iris plane appears rather flat for an eye with angle-closure glaucoma. This suspicion can be confirmed with ultrasound biomicroscopy. The ophthalmologist should also suspect plateau iris if angle closure occurs in younger myopic patients.

An iridectomy is performed to remove any component of pupillary block; this treatment is sufficient for eyes with *plateau iris configuration,* the more common manifestation. However, even after iridectomy, a few eyes with *plateau iris syndrome* will develop angle closure if the pupil is dilated. These patients should be treated with long-term miotic therapy. Laser peripheral iridoplasty to thin the peripheral iris may be required in some individuals with this condition (Fig VIII-3).

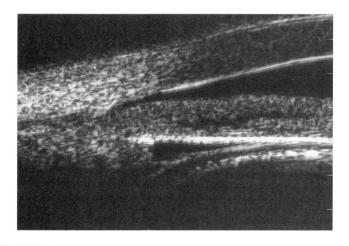

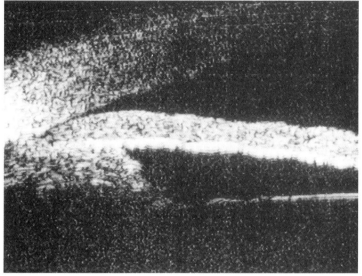

FIG VIII-2—Ultrasound biomicroscopy images of a plateau iris. (Photographs courtesy of Charles J. Pavlin, MD.)

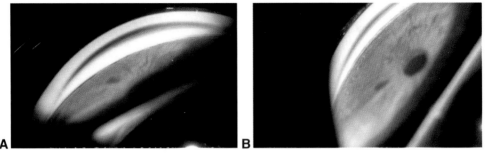

FIG VIII-3—*A,* Plateau iris syndrome with a flat iris plane and closed angle. *B,* Plateau iris syndrome with an open angle following laser peripheral iridoplasty.

Secondary Angle-Closure Glaucoma with Pupillary Block

Lens-Induced Angle-Closure Glaucoma

Intumescent lenses or dislocated lenses (complete zonular dehiscence) may increase pupillary block and cause angle-closure glaucoma. Angle closure from a swollen lens is sometimes referred to as *phacomorphic glaucoma.* With lens subluxation (partial zonular dehiscence), as in Marfan syndrome or homocystinuria, pupillary block may be intermittent and vitreous may contribute to it. Laser iridotomy is the treatment of choice, as it is with primary angle-closure glaucoma with pupillary block. Lens extraction is indicated if pupillary block is not relieved or when the anterior chamber progressively shallows following laser iridotomy.

Microsphorophakia, a congenital disorder in which the lens has a spherical or globular shape, may cause pupillary block and angle-closure glaucoma. Treatment with cycloplegia may flatten the lens and pull it posteriorly, breaking the pupillary block; miotics may make the glaucoma worse. Microsphorophakia is often familial and may occur as an isolated condition or as part of either Weill-Marchesani or Marfan syndrome.

Uveitis can cause posterior synechiae to the lens, preventing posterior chamber aqueous humor from flowing into the anterior chamber. The peripheral iris balloons forward, resulting in *iris bombé* and occluding the trabecular meshwork.

Pupillary block may occur in *aphakic* and *pseudophakic* eyes. An intact vitreous face can block the pupil and/or an iridectomy in aphakic or pseudophakic eyes or in phakic eyes with dislocated lenses. Generally, the anterior chamber shallows and the iris demonstrates considerable bombé. Treatment with mydriatic and cycloplegic agents, beta-adrenergic antagonists, carbonic anhydrase inhibitors, and hyperosmotic agents may restore the aqueous flow through the pupil. One or more laser iridotomies may be required.

A variant of this problem occurs with *anterior chamber intraocular lenses.* Pupillary block develops with apposition of the iris, vitreous face, and lens optic. The lens haptic may obstruct the iridectomy. The peripheral iris bows forward around the anterior chamber IOL to occlude the chamber angle. The central chamber remains deep in this instance, because the lens haptic and optic prevent the central portions of the iris and vitreous face from moving forward. Laser iridotomies, often multiple, are required to relieve the block.

Pupillary block may occur after *extracapsular cataract extraction* when an iridectomy has not been performed at the time of surgery. Although not common, this complication can occur when the iris forms adhesions to a posterior chamber IOL or to the posterior capsule. Pupillary block may also occur following posterior capsulotomy when vitreous obstructs the pupil. A peripheral iridectomy should be done after rupture of the posterior capsule with or without vitreous loss during cataract surgery.

See also BCSC Section 11, *Lens and Cataract.*

Nonrhegmatogenous retinal detachment may occur from subretinal effusion where no retinal breaks are present. Retinoblastoma, Coats disease, metastatic carcinoma, choroidal melanoma, and subretinal neovascularization in age-related macular degeneration with extensive effusion or hemorrhage are associated with this condition. The subretinal fluid or hemorrhage may rapidly accumulate, and it can push the bullous retinal detachment forward to a retrolenticular position and flatten the anterior chamber completely. With a *Y-suture retinal detachment,* the retina may be dramatically visible behind the lens in a slit-lamp examination. In a *rhegmatogenous retinal detachment,* the subretinal fluid can escape through the retinal tear and equalize the hydraulic pressure on both sides of the retina. By contrast, in a nonrhegmatogenous retinal detachment, the subretinal fluid accumulates and progressively pushes the retina forward against the lens like a hydraulic press. The creation of a retinotomy, like an iridotomy in acute angle-closure glaucoma, relieves the increased IOP by equalizing the hydraulic pressure in front of and behind the retina and allows the retina to fall back into the vitreous cavity.

Secondary Angle-Closure Glaucoma Without Pupillary Block

Diseases in this category may occur through one of two mechanisms:

□ Contraction of a membrane, band, or exudate in the angle, leading to peripheral anterior synechiae

□ Forward displacement of the lens–iris diaphragm, often accompanied by swelling and anterior rotation of the ciliary body

Previous Pupillary Block

Failure to relieve pupillary-block glaucoma promptly can result in permanent synechial closure of the angle and chronic glaucoma. The severity of the glaucoma depends on the extent of closure and the functioning of the remaining angle.

Flat Anterior Chamber

A flat anterior chamber from any cause can result in the formation of PAS. Debate continues concerning how long a postoperative flat chamber should be treated conservatively before surgical intervention is undertaken. Hypotony in an eye with a postoperative flat chamber often indicates a wound leak. A Seidel test should be performed to locate the leak. Simple pressure patching or bandage contact lens application will often cause the leak to seal and the chamber to re-form. If the chamber does not re-form, it should be repaired surgically to prevent permanent synechial closure of the angle.

Some ophthalmologists repair the wound leak and re-form a flat chamber following cataract surgery within 24 hours. Others prefer corticosteroid therapy for several days to prevent synechiae formation. If the hyaloid face or an IOL is in contact with the cornea, the chambers should be re-formed without delay to minimize corneal endothelial damage. Early intervention should also be considered in the presence of corneal edema, excessive inflammation, or posterior synechiae formation.

Neovascular Glaucoma

Many disorders result in the development of neovascularization of the iris and neovascular glaucoma (Table VIII-2). Almost all of these disorders are characterized by retinal hypoxia and retinal capillary nonperfusion, the same factors involved in the development of retinal neovascularization. Rarely, anterior segment neovascularization may occur without demonstrable retinal ischemia, as in heterochromic iridocyclitis and other types of uveitis, exfoliation syndrome, or isolated iris melanomas. When an ocular cause cannot be found, carotid artery obstructive disease should be considered. Histologically, neovascularization of the iris consists of a fibrovascular membrane that may overgrow the iris and trabecular meshwork. Initially, the fibrovascular tissue itself lines an otherwise open anterior chamber angle. With time, however, the neovascular tissue may contract to form PAS. The synechial closure can develop over a period of days. In establishing a correct diagnosis, it is important to distinguish dilated iris vessels associated with inflammation from newly formed abnormal blood vessels (see Fig VI-7, page 35).

TABLE VIII-2

DISORDERS PREDISPOSING TO NEOVASCULARIZATION OF THE IRIS AND ANGLE

Systemic vascular disease	*Other ocular disease*
Carotid occlusive disease*	Chronic uveitis
Carotid artery ligation	Chronic retinal detachment
Carotid cavernous fistula	Endophthalmitis
Giant cell arteritis	Stickler syndrome
Takayasu (pulseless) disease	Retinoschisis
Ocular vascular disease	*Intraocular tumors*
Diabetic retinopathy*	Uveal melanoma
Central retinal vein occlusion*	Metastatic carcinoma
Central retinal artery occlusion	Retinoblastoma
Branch retinal vein occlusion	Reticulum cell sarcoma
Sickle cell retinopathy	
Coats disease	*Ocular therapy*
Eales disease	Postvitrectomy in diabetes
Retinopathy of prematurity	Radiation therapy
Persistent hyperplastic primary vitreous	
Syphilitic vasculitis	*Trauma*
Anterior segment ischemia	

*most common causes

Because therapy for neovascular glaucoma has a relatively low success rate, prevention is desirable. The most common cause of iris neovascularization is ischemic retinopathy, and retinal therapy should be performed whenever possible. The treatment of choice when the ocular media are clear is panretinal photocoagulation; when cloudy media prevent laser therapy, panretinal cryotherapy is preferred. Frequently, marked involution of the neovascularization occurs. The resulting decrease in neovascularization after retinal ablation may reduce or cure the glaucoma if total synechial closure has not yet occurred. Furthermore, even in the presence of total synechial angle closure, panretinal photocoagulation may improve the success rate of filtering surgery by eliminating the angiogenic stimulus.

Medical therapy is usually ineffective in controlling IOP when the outflow system has been occluded. However, topical beta-adrenergic antagonists, cycloplegics, and corticosteroids may be useful in reducing IOP and decreasing inflammation. Filtering surgery has a better chance of success once neovascularization has regressed after panretinal photocoagulation. A variety of tube-shunt operations and pharmacological manipulations of wound healing (e.g., 5-fluorouracil and mitomycin-C) have been proposed for this situation. When other measures fail, a cyclodestructive procedure may help reduce IOP.

Iridocorneal Endothelial (ICE) Syndrome

Glaucoma is an important feature of the iridocorneal endothelial (ICE) syndrome. Included in this syndrome are several apparently related disorders, including progressive iris atrophy, iris nevus (Cogan-Reese) syndrome, and Chandler syndrome. All involve a disorder of the corneal endothelium with varying degrees of endothelialization of the anterior chamber angle and iris surface. Progressive iris atrophy is characterized by marked corectopia, iris stromal and pigment epithelial atrophy, and hole formation. The iris nevus syndrome is distinguished by nodular or diffuse pigmented lesions on the anterior iris surface. Iris changes in Chandler syndrome are minimal or absent, but dysfunction of the corneal endothelium results in corneal edema, often at normal IOP levels.

Because many patients present with findings of more than one of these disorders, the ICE syndrome is now thought to represent a disease spectrum (Fig VIII-4). This syndrome is almost always unilateral with a higher prevalence in women. While development of PAS is common in the ICE syndrome, the glaucoma is frequently more advanced than the extent of the synechiae would indicate, presumably because of the angle endothelialization. The possibility that the etiology of the ICE syndrome may be a result of a herpesvirus infection has been raised.

Tumors

Tumors in the posterior segment of the eye or anterior uveal cysts may force the lens–iris diaphragm forward and cause angle-closure glaucoma. The most common type of tumors causing angle-closure glaucoma are uveal melanomas. Extensive tumors of the posterior pole may also cause neovascular glaucoma.

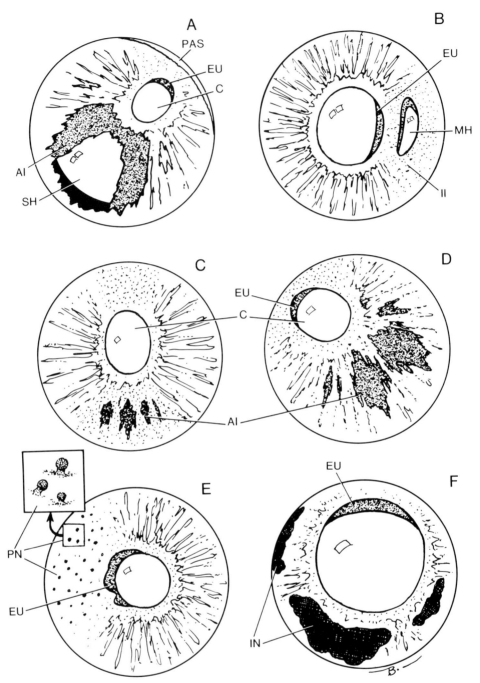

FIG VIII-4—The spectrum of iris abnormalities in the iridocorneal endothelial syndrome. *A,* Progressive iris atrophy with peripheral anterior synechiae *(PAS)* visible on peripheral cornea, marked corectopia *(C),* ectropion uveae *(EU)* and a stretch hole *(SH)* surrounded by atrophic iris *(AI).* *B,* Progressive iris atrophy with a melting hole *(MH)* surrounded by ischemic iris *(II).* *C,* Chandler syndrome with mild corectopia and atrophy of the iris. *D,* Intermediate variation with more advanced corectopia and atrophy of the iris than in the typical Chandler syndrome, but no hole in the iris. *E* and *F,* Cogan-Reese (iris nevus) syndrome with pigmented, pedunculated nodules *(PN)* or diffuse iris nevi *(IN).* (Reproduced with permission from Shields MB. *Textbook of Glaucoma.* 3rd ed. Baltimore: Williams & Wilkins; 1992.)

Inflammation

Secondary angle-closure glaucoma resulting from inflammation may occur by one of three mechanisms:

- □ Posterior synechiae may cause a secluded pupil, iris bombé, and angle-closure glaucoma. The pupillary block in iris bombé must be relieved quickly by iridectomy in order to prevent permanent damage to the trabecular meshwork.
- □ Organization of inflammatory exudates in the chamber angle may pull the peripheral iris forward, producing PAS.
- □ Ischemia secondary to inflammation may, rarely, cause rubeosis iridis and neovascular glaucoma.

Ocular inflammation can lead to the shallowing and closure of the anterior chamber angle by uveal effusion, resulting in anterior rotation of the ciliary body. Significant posterior uveitis causing massive exudative retinal detachment may lead to angle-closure glaucoma through forward displacement of the lens–iris diaphragm. Treatment is primarily directed at the underlying cause of uveitis. Aqueous suppressants and corticosteroids are the primary agents for reducing elevated IOP and preventing synechial angle closure.

Interstitial keratitis may be associated with open-angle or angle-closure glaucoma. The angle closure may be caused by chronic inflammation and PAS formation or by multiple cysts of the iris pigment epithelium.

Ciliary-Block Glaucoma

Ciliary-block glaucoma is also known as malignant glaucoma, aqueous misdirection, and posterior aqueous diversion syndrome. It results from misdirection of aqueous humor into the vitreous cavity and occurs most commonly after intraocular surgery in eyes with prior angle-closure glaucoma. It may also occur in eyes with open angles following cataract surgery or various laser procedures and can even occur spontaneously. The posterior flow of aqueous humor into the vitreous displaces the lens–iris diaphragm anteriorly, causing the central and peripheral anterior chamber to become very shallow. This condition usually occurs soon after glaucoma surgery, especially when cycloplegics are stopped or miotics instituted; however, ciliary block may also develop years later.

Ciliary-block glaucoma is characterized by a shallow anterior chamber and elevated IOP. It must be differentiated from choroidal separation, pupillary block, and suprachoroidal hemorrhage. Medical treatment includes intensive cycloplegic and mydriatic therapy, beta-adrenergic antagonists, alpha$_2$-adrenergic agonists, carbonic anhydrase inhibitors, and hyperosmotic agents. Miotics make ciliary-block glaucoma worse. In aphakic and pseudophakic eyes, the anterior vitreous can be treated with the Nd:YAG laser. Argon laser photocoagulation of the ciliary processes has reportedly been helpful in treating this condition; this procedure may alter the adjacent vitreous face. The surgical treatment is vitreous surgery combined with anterior chamber deepening.

Lundy DC. Ciliary block glaucoma. In: *Focal Points: Clinical Modules for Ophthalmologists*. San Francisco: American Academy of Ophthalmology; 1999;17:3.

Epithelial and Fibrous Downgrowth

Epithelial downgrowth occurs when surface epithelium grows into the eye through a penetrating wound, such as a fistula following intraocular surgery. The epithelium forms a membrane that may cover the corneal endothelium, trabecular meshwork, iris, ciliary processes, and vitreous. The leading edge of this membrane may be seen by slit-lamp examination. Severe secondary glaucoma may result. The argon laser produces characteristic white burns of the epithelial membrane on the iris surface, which may help indicate the diagnosis of epithelial downgrowth and determine the extent of involvement. If the diagnosis is in question, it may be confirmed by cytological examination of aqueous aspirate. Radical surgery is recommended to remove the intraocular epithelial membrane and the affected tissues and to repair the fistula, but the prognosis remains poor.

Fibrovascular tissue may also proliferate into an eye from a penetrating wound. While generally not as aggressive as epithelial downgrowth, *fibrous downgrowth* can also cause corneal decompensation and secondary glaucoma. Medication is the preferred treatment of the secondary glaucoma, although surgical intervention may be required. See chapter XI, Medical Management of Glaucoma, and chapter XII, Surgical Therapy of Glaucoma, for detailed discussion.

Trauma

Angle-closure glaucoma without pupillary block may develop following ocular trauma from peripheral anterior synechiae associated with angle recession or from contusion, hyphema, and inflammation.

Retinal Surgery and Retinal Vascular Disease

Angle-closure glaucoma may occur following treatment of retinal disorders. Scleral buckling operations, especially encircling bands, can produce shallowing of the anterior chamber angle and frank angle-closure glaucoma, often accompanied by choroidal effusion and anterior rotation of the ciliary body, causing a plateau iris configuration with a relatively deep central anterior chamber. For this reason, it is important to measure IOP after retinal detachment surgery. Usually, the anterior chamber deepens over days to weeks with therapy of cycloplegics, anti-inflammatory agents, beta-adrenergic antagonists, carbonic anhydrase inhibitors, and hyperosmotic agents.

If medical management is unsuccessful, argon laser gonioplasty, drainage of suprachoroidal fluid, or adjustment of the buckle is required. The scleral buckle should be shifted if it is compromising a vortex vein. Iridectomy is usually of little benefit in this condition. Following pars plana vitreous surgery, angle-closure glaucoma through the pupillary-block mechanism may result from the injection of air, long-acting gases such as sulfur hexafluoride and perfluorocarbons (perfluoropropane and perfluoroethane), or silicone oil into the vitreous cavity to tamponade the retina. These substances are less dense than water and rise to the top of the eye. When these substances have been used, an iridectomy may be beneficial; it should be located inferiorly.

After panretinal photocoagulation, IOP may become elevated by an angle-closure mechanism. The ciliary body is thickened and rotated, and often an anterior annular choroidal detachment occurs. Generally, this secondary glaucoma is self-limited, and therapy is directed at temporary medical management with cycloplegic agents, topical corticosteroids, and aqueous suppressants.

Central retinal vein occlusion (CRVO) sometimes causes early shallowing of the chamber angle, presumably because of swelling of the choroid and ciliary body. In rare cases the angle becomes sufficiently compromised to cause angle-closure glaucoma. The chamber deepens and the glaucoma resolves over one to several weeks. Medical therapy of the glaucoma is usually preferred; gonioplasty and iridectomy are reserved for unresponsive patients. However, if the contralateral eye of a patient with CRVO has a potentially occludable anterior chamber angle, the ophthalmologist must consider an underlying pupillary-block mechanism and the possible need for bilateral iridectomy.

Nanophthalmos

In nanophthalmos the eye is normal in shape but unusually small. A nanophthalmic eye has a shortened anteroposterior diameter, a small corneal diameter, and a relatively large lens for the eye volume. Thickened sclera may impede drainage from the vortex veins. These eyes are markedly hyperopic and highly susceptible to angle-closure glaucoma. Intraocular surgery is frequently complicated by choroidal effusion and nonrhegmatogenous retinal detachment. Choroidal effusion may occur spontaneously, and it can induce angle-closure glaucoma. Argon laser peripheral iridoplasty, laser iridotomy, and medical therapy are the safest ways to manage glaucoma in these patients.

Fuchs Corneal Endothelial Dystrophy

Eyes with Fuchs corneal endothelial dystrophy and shallow anterior chamber angles may develop angle-closure glaucoma caused by a gradual thickening of the cornea from edema, resulting in eventual closure of the anterior chamber angle.

Retinopathy of Prematurity

Contracting retrolental tissue seen in retinopathy of prematurity (retrolental fibroplasia) and persistent hyperplastic primary vitreous (PHPV) can cause progressive shallowing of the anterior chamber angle with subsequent angle-closure glaucoma. In retinopathy of prematurity the onset of this complication usually occurs at 3–6 months of age during the cicatricial phase of the disease. However, the angle-closure glaucoma may occur later in childhood.

PHPV is usually unilateral and often associated with microphthalmos and elongated ciliary processes. The contracture of the hyperplastic primary vitreous and swelling of a cataractous lens may result in subsequent angle-closure glaucoma.

Epstein DL, Allingham RR, Schuman JS, eds. *Chandler and Grant's Glaucoma.* 4th ed. Baltimore: Williams & Wilkins; 1997.

Hoskins HD Jr, Kass MA, eds. *Becker-Shaffer's Diagnosis and Therapy of the Glaucomas.* 6th ed. St. Louis: CV Mosby Co; 1989.

Ritch R, Shields MB, Krupin T, eds. *The Glaucomas.* vols 1 and 2. St. Louis: CV Mosby Co; 1989.

Shields MB. *Textbook of Glaucoma.* 3rd ed. Baltimore: Williams & Wilkins; 1992.

CHAPTER IX

Combined-Mechanism Glaucoma

Combined-mechanism glaucoma occurs when a combination of two or more forms of glaucoma present either sequentially or simultaneously. This situation may occur following a primary acute angle-closure glaucoma attack, when IOP remains elevated after a peripheral iridectomy in spite of an open and normal-appearing anterior chamber angle. Combined-mechanism glaucoma can also appear in a patient with open-angle glaucoma who develops partial angle closure from other causes. Examples include a patient with open-angle glaucoma who develops angle closure as a result of miotic therapy or a patient with pseudophakic open-angle glaucoma who develops peripheral anterior synechiae after an episode of pupillary block.

IOP elevation can occur as a result of either or both of the following:

☐ The intrinsic resistance of the trabecular meshwork to aqueous outflow in open-angle glaucoma

☐ The direct anatomic obstruction of the filtering meshwork by synechiae in angle-closure glaucoma

Treatment is modified based on the proportion of open angle to closed angle and the etiology of the angle-closure component.

CHAPTER X

Childhood Glaucoma

Definitions and Classification

Primary congenital or *infantile glaucoma* is evident either at birth or within the first few years of life. Both conditions are believed to be caused by dysplasia of the anterior chamber angle without other ocular or systemic abnormalities. *Secondary infantile glaucoma* is associated with inflammatory, neoplastic, hamartomatous, metabolic, or other congenital abnormalities of the eye. *Juvenile glaucoma* is recognized later in childhood (after 3 years of age) or in early adulthood when the eye no longer expands in response to elevated IOP.

The term *developmental glaucoma* includes primary congenital glaucoma and glaucoma associated with other developmental anomalies, either ocular or systemic. Glaucoma associated with other ocular or systemic abnormalities may be inherited or acquired. The term *buphthalmos* (cow's eye) refers to enlargement of the globe. This condition appears when the onset of elevated IOP occurs before the age of 3 in primary congenital or infantile glaucoma or in the pediatric glaucomas associated with other ocular and/or systemic abnormalities.

Epidemiology and Genetics

Glaucoma in the pediatric age group is heterogeneous. Isolated congenital glaucoma accounts for approximately 50%–70% of the congenital glaucomas and occurs much less frequently than primary adult glaucoma; primary infantile glaucoma is believed to be rare. Of pediatric glaucoma cases, 60% are diagnosed by the age of 6 months and 80% within the first year of life. Approximately 65% of patients are male, and involvement is bilateral in 70% of all cases.

Although some pedigrees suggest an autosomal dominant inheritance, most patients show a recessive pattern with incomplete or variable penetrance and possibly multifactorial inheritance. Some types of juvenile glaucoma that have an autosomal dominant inheritance pattern have been mapped to chromosome 1q21–31. Some cases of primary congenital glaucoma have been associated with chromosomal rearrangement. The natural history of this disorder is variable; in the worst case, prior to effective surgical therapy, the disease almost always resulted in blindness.

Some patients with congenital, infantile, or juvenile glaucoma may have Axenfeld-Rieger syndrome, aniridia, or a multisystem genetic disorder. All pediatric patients with glaucoma or adults who had glaucoma in childhood should be evaluated by a geneticist for counseling purposes.

Clinical Features

Characteristic findings of infantile glaucoma include the classic triad of presenting symptoms in the newborn: *epiphora, photophobia,* and *blepharospasm.* Diagnosis of infantile glaucoma depends on careful clinical evaluation, including IOP measurement, measurement of corneal diameter, gonioscopy, measurement of axial length by ultrasonography, and ophthalmoscopy.

External eye examination may reveal buphthalmos with corneal enlargement greater than 12 mm in diameter during the first year of life. (The normal horizontal corneal diameter is 10.0–10.5 mm in full-term newborns and smaller in premature newborns.) Corneal edema may range from mild haze to dense opacification of the corneal stroma because of elevated IOP. Corneal edema is present in 25% of affected infants at birth and in more than 60% by the sixth month. Tears in Descemet's membrane, called Haab's striae, may occur acutely as a result of corneal stretching and are typically oriented horizontally or concentric to the limbus.

Reduced visual acuity may occur as a result of optic atrophy, corneal clouding, astigmatism, amblyopia, cataract, lens dislocation, or retinal detachment. Amblyopia may be caused by the corneal opacity itself or by refractive error. The enlargement of the eye causes myopia, while tears in Descemet's membrane can cause a large astigmatism. Appropriate measures to prevent or treat amblyopia should be initiated as early as possible.

It is possible for the clinician to measure the IOP in some infants under age 6 months without general anesthesia or sedation by performing the measurement while the infant is feeding or asleep following feeding. However, critical evaluation of infants requires an examination under anesthesia. Most general anesthetic agents and sedatives lower IOP. In addition, infants may become dehydrated in preparation for general anesthesia, also reducing the IOP. As anesthesia becomes deeper, IOP falls. The only exception to this rule is ketamine, which may raise IOP. Normal IOP in an infant under anesthesia may range from 10 to 20 mm Hg, depending upon the tonometer. A significant IOP elevation may occur in only one eye in 25%–30% of cases.

In isolated childhood glaucoma the anterior chamber is characteristically deep with normal iris structure. Gonioscopy under anesthesia, using a direct gonioscopic lens, is recommended. The normal anterior chamber angle in childhood is different from that in adulthood. Findings include a high and flat iris insertion, absence of angle recess, peripheral iris hypoplasia, tenting of the peripheral iris pigment epithelium, and thickened uveal trabecular meshwork. The angle is typically open with a high insertion of the iris root that forms a scalloped line as a result of abnormal tissue with a shagreened, glistening appearance. This tissue holds the peripheral iris anteriorly. The angle is usually avascular, but loops of vessels from the major arterial circle may be seen above the iris root.

Many of these findings are nonspecific, and it may be difficult to distinguish the gonioscopic findings in infantile glaucoma from a normal infant angle. If corneal edema prevents an adequate view of the angle, the epithelium may be removed with a scalpel blade or a cotton-tipped applicator soaked in 70% alcohol to improve visibility.

Visualization of the optic disc may be facilitated by using a direct ophthalmoscope and a direct gonioscopic or fundus lens on the cornea. The optic nerve head of a normal infant is pink with a small physiologic cup. Glaucomatous cupping in childhood resembles the cupping in adulthood, with preferential loss of neural tissue in the superior and inferior poles. In childhood the scleral canal enlarges in response to elevated IOP, causing enlargement of the cup. Cupping may be reversible if IOP is lowered, and progressive cupping indicates poor control of IOP.

Photographic documentation of the optic disc is recommended. Ultrasonography may be useful in documenting progression of glaucoma by recording increasing axial length. Increased axial length may be reversible following reduction of IOP.

Pathophysiology

Because histopathological findings in infantile glaucoma vary, many theories of pathogenesis have been proposed. These theories fall into two main groups. Some investigators have proposed that a cellular or membranous abnormality in the trabecular meshwork is the primary pathological mechanism. This abnormality is described as either an anomalous impermeable trabecular meshwork or a Barkan membrane covering the trabecular meshwork. Other investigators have emphasized a more widespread anterior segment anomaly, including abnormal insertion of the ciliary muscle. While the exact mechanism of primary infantile glaucoma remains unproven, there is little doubt that the disease represents a developmental anomaly of the angle structures. Many of its features suggest a developmental arrest in the late embryonic period.

Differential Diagnosis

Differential diagnosis of infantile glaucoma includes many other conditions with similar features (Table X-1). Excessive tearing may be caused by an obstruction of the lacrimal drainage system. Ocular abnormalities associated with enlarged corneas include X-linked congenital megalocornea without glaucoma. Tears in Descemet's membrane resulting from birth trauma, often associated with forceps-assisted deliveries, are usually vertical or oblique. Corneal opacification and clouding have many possible causes:

- Birth trauma
- Dysgeneses (Peters anomaly and sclerocornea)
- Dystrophies (congenital hereditary endothelial dystrophy and posterior polymorphous dystrophy)
- Choristomas (dermoid and dermislike choristoma)
- Intrauterine inflammation (congenital syphilis and rubella)
- Inborn errors of metabolism (mucopolysaccharidoses and cystinosis)
- Keratomalacia
- Skin disorders that affect the cornea (congenital ichthyosis and congenital dyskeratosis)

TABLE X-1

DIAGNOSTIC CONSIDERATIONS FOR SYMPTOMS AND SIGNS OF INFANTILE GLAUCOMA

Excessive tearing
    Nasolacrimal duct obstruction
    Corneal epithelial defect or abrasion
    Conjunctivitis

Corneal enlargement or apparent enlargement
    X-linked megalocornea
    High myopia
    Exophthalmos
    Shallow orbits (e.g., craniofacial dysostoses)

Corneal clouding
    Birth trauma
    Inflammatory corneal disease
    Congenital hereditary corneal dystrophies
    Corneal malformations (dermoid tumors, sclerocornea)
    Keratomalacia
    Metabolic disorders with associated corneal abnormalities (mucopolysaccharidoses, corneal lipidosis, cystinosis, and von Gierke disease)
    Skin disorders affecting the cornea (congenital ichthyosis and congenital dyskeratosis)
    Optic nerve abnormalities (optic nerve pit, optic nerve coloboma, optic nerve hypoplasia, physiologic cupping)

Long-term Prognosis and Follow-up

Medications have limited long-term value for congenital and infantile glaucoma in most cases, and the preferred therapy is surgical. The initial procedures of choice are goniotomy if the cornea is clear and trabeculotomy ab externo if the cornea is hazy. The success rates are similar for both procedures. Trabeculectomy and shunt procedures should be reserved for those cases where goniotomy or trabeculotomy has failed.

As temporizing therapy prior to surgery, miotics, beta-adrenergic antagonists, or carbonic anhydrase inhibitors may be used to control IOP and help clear a cloudy cornea. These drugs must be used with caution and at doses appropriate for the child's weight to prevent systemic side effects. The parents should be instructed in particular to occlude the nasolacrimal drainage system for at least 2 minutes immediately after administering topical beta-adrenergic antagonists and to be alert for apnea. Young children on carbonic anhydrase inhibitors require assessment for possible acidosis, hypokalemia, and feeding problems.

Long-term prognosis has greatly improved with the development of effective surgical techniques, particularly for patients who are asymptomatic at birth and present with onset of symptoms before 24 months of age. When symptoms are present at birth or when the disease is diagnosed after 24 months of age, the outlook for surgical control of IOP is more guarded. Even patients whose IOP is usually controlled by surgery may experience late complications such as amblyopia, corneal scarring, strabismus, anisometropia, cataract, lens subluxation, susceptibility of an eye with a thinned sclera to trauma, and recurrent glaucoma in the affected or unaffected eye many years later.

Developmental Glaucomas with Associated Anomalies

Glaucoma may be associated with other ocular abnormalities, including the following conditions:

□ Microphthalmos

□ Corneal anomalies (microcornea, cornea plana, sclerocornea)

□ Anterior segment dysgenesis (Axenfeld-Rieger syndrome and Peters syndrome)

□ Aniridia

□ Lens anomalies (dislocation, microspherophakia)

□ Persistent hyperplastic primary vitreous

Glaucoma may occur in multisystem syndromes.

Developmental glaucoma with either an open or a closed angle may be associated with other anomalies. Some important anomalies include syndromes with known chromosomal abnormalities, systemic disorders of unknown etiology, and ocular congenital disorders. Glaucomas associated with congenital anomalies are summarized in Table X-2.

A number of systemic disorders are also associated with pediatric glaucoma. These include the following:

□ Sturge-Weber syndrome

□ Neurofibromatosis

□ Marfan syndrome

□ Homocystinuria

□ Weill-Marchesani syndrome

With Sturge-Weber syndrome and neurofibromatosis in particular, upper eyelid involvement is associated with an increased risk of glaucoma. A number of these conditions have ocular findings similar to primary infantile glaucoma; in others, the glaucoma is secondary.

Secondary glaucoma may develop in infants and children from any cause seen in adults. These include trauma, inflammation, retinopathy of prematurity with secondary angle-closure glaucoma, lens-induced glaucoma, corticosteroid-induced glaucoma, pigmentary glaucoma, and glaucoma secondary to intraocular tumors. Retinoblastoma, juvenile xanthogranuloma, and medulloepithelioma are some of the intraocular tumors known to lead to secondary glaucoma in infants and children. Rubella and congenital cataract are also important associated conditions. Clinicians now realize that children often develop glaucoma within 3 years following surgery for congenital cataract.

BCSC Section 6, *Pediatric Ophthalmology and Strabismus.*

Higginbotham EJ, Lee DA, eds. *Management of Difficult Glaucoma: A Clinician's Guide.* London: Blackwell Scientific Publications; 1994.

Hoskins HD Jr, Kass MA, eds. *Becker-Shaffer's Diagnosis and Therapy of the Glaucomas.* 6th ed. St Louis: CV Mosby Co; 1989.

Isenberg SJ, ed. *The Eye in Infancy.* 2nd ed. St Louis: Mosby–Year Book; 1994.

Lee DA, ed. New developments in glaucoma. *Ophthalmol Clin North Am.* Philadelphia: WB Saunders Co; 1995;8:2.

Shields MB. *Textbook of Glaucoma.* 3rd ed. Baltimore: Williams & Wilkins; 1992.

Tasman W, Jaeger EA, eds. *Duane's Clinical Ophthalmology.* Philadelphia: JB Lippincott Co; 1992.

TABLE X-2

ANOMALIES ASSOCIATED WITH CHILDHOOD GLAUCOMAS

Glaucoma associated with systemic congenital syndromes, with reported chromosomal abnormalities

Trisomy 21 (Down syndrome, trisomy G syndrome)
Mental deficiency, short stature, cardiac anomalies, hypotonia, atypical facies

Trisomy 13 (Patau syndrome)
Mental retardation, deafness, heart disease, motor seizures

Trisomy 18 (Edwards syndrome, trisomy E syndrome)
Low-set ears, high-arched hard palate, ventricular septal defects, rocker-bottom feet, short sternum, hypertonia

Turner (XO/XX) syndrome
Short stature, postadolescent females with sexual infantilism, webbed neck, mental retardation, congenital deafness, multiple systemic anomalies

Glaucoma associated with systemic congenital disorders

Lowe (oculocerebrorenal) syndrome
X-linked recessive disease, mental retardation, renal rickets, aminoaciduria, hypotonia, acidemia, cataracts

Stickler syndrome (hereditary progressive arthro-ophthalmopathy)
Autosomal dominant connective tissue dysplasia, ocular, orofacial, and generalized skeletal abnormalities with high myopia, open-angle glaucoma, cataracts, vitreoretinal degeneration, retinal detachment

Zellweger (cerebrohepatorenal) syndrome
Congenital autosomal recessive syndrome, abnormal facies, cerebral dysgenesis, hepatic interstitial fibrosis, polycystic kidneys, central nervous system abnormalities
Ocular findings: nystagmus, corneal clouding, cataracts, retinal vascular and pigmentary abnormalities, optic nerve head lesions

Hallermann-Streiff syndrome (dyscephalic mandibulo-oculofacial syndrome, François dyscephalic syndrome)
Micrognathia, dwarfism, microphthalmos, cataract, aniridia, optic atrophy

Rubinstein-Taybi (broad-thumb) syndrome
Mental and motor retardation, typical congenital skeletal deformities of large thumbs and first toes
Ocular findings: bushy brows, hypertelorism, epicanthus, anti-mongoloid slant of eyelids, hyperopia, strabismus

Oculodentodigital dysplasia (Meyer-Schwickerath and Weyers syndrome)
Autosomal dominant inheritance, hypoplastic dental enamel, microdontia, bilateral syndactyly, thin nose, microcornea, microphthalmos

TABLE X-2

Glaucoma associated with systemic congenital disorders (continued)

Prader-Willi syndrome
Chromosome 15 deletion, muscular hypotonia, hypogonadism, obesity, mental retardation
Ocular findings: Ocular albinism, congenital ectropion uveae, iris stromal hypoplasia, angle abnormalities

Cockayne syndrome
Autosomal recessive disorder, dwarfism, mental retardation, progressive wasting, "birdlike" facies
Ocular findings: retinal degeneration, cataracts, corneal exposure, blepharitis, nystagmus, hypoplastic irides, irregular pupils

Fetal alcohol syndrome
Teratogenic effects of alcohol during gestation, facial abnormalities, mental retardation, anterior segment involvement resembling Axenfeld-Rieger syndrome and Peters anomaly, optic nerve hypoplasia

Glaucoma associated with ocular congenital disorders

Congenital ectropion uveae
Congenital corneal staphyloma
Cornea plana
Iridoschisis
Megalocornea
Microcoria
Microcornea
Microphthalmos
Morning glory syndrome
Persistent hyperplastic primary vitreous (PHPV)
Retinopathy of prematurity
Sclerocornea

CHAPTER XI

Medical Management of Glaucoma

Two problems arise in choosing an appropriate glaucoma therapy: when to treat and how to treat. Primary angle-closure and infantile glaucoma are treated as soon as the diagnosis is made. Open-angle glaucoma is treated when damage to the optic nerve has been demonstrated in the form of progressive pathologic cupping and/or characteristic visual field defects, or when pressure is elevated to an extent that is likely to cause damage to the optic nerve.

The risks of therapy must always be weighed against the anticipated benefits. A patient with early open-angle glaucoma is difficult to distinguish from a glaucoma suspect. Since the latter has a relatively small risk of ultimate ocular damage, the decision of when to treat the glaucoma suspect who has not demonstrated actual nerve damage remains controversial. Most authorities agree that treatment of the glaucoma suspect should be limited to those patients with a high risk of damage to the optic nerve. Such patients have risk factors that include markedly elevated IOP, a positive family history of glaucoma, myopia, diabetes mellitus, cardiovascular disease, and asymmetric cupping. Black patients are also at higher risk.

The goal of glaucoma management is to preserve visual function by lowering IOP below a level that is likely to produce further damage to the optic nerve. Generally speaking, the treatment regimen that achieves this goal with the lowest risk, fewest side effects, and least disruption of the patient's life should be the one employed. The anticipated benefits of any therapeutic regimen should justify the risks. Regimens associated with substantial side effects should be reserved for patients with a high risk of eventual severe visual dysfunction. For example, it is reasonable to expose a patient to the side effects of systemic carbonic anhydrase inhibitors (CAIs) when significant damage to the visual field and optic nerve has occurred and the elevated IOP is not controlled by less toxic medications. However, the physician should exercise caution in subjecting a patient to the risk of the significant side effects of these agents when progressive visual field loss or cupping has not been established.

The interrelationship between medical and surgical therapy is complex. The treatment of pupillary-block angle-closure glaucoma and infantile glaucoma is primarily surgical, either laser or incisional, with medical therapy taking a secondary role. Initial treatment of primary open-angle glaucoma has commonly been medical, with surgery undertaken only if medical treatment fails or is not well tolerated. However, this assumption is currently under study; in some cases initial surgery may prove more beneficial. Surgical therapy is discussed in detail in the following chapter.

Treatment of secondary glaucoma is comparable to treatment of the primary glaucoma that it most closely resembles. In any event, therapy should progress from the less dangerous to the more dangerous, and then only when the initial treatments fail and the risk of severe visual dysfunction is high. In addition, the efficacy of the therapeutic regimen should be periodically reevaluated.

Medical Agents

Antiglaucoma agents are divided into several groups based on chemical structure and pharmacologic action. There are five groups of agents in common clinical use:

☐ Beta-adrenergic antagonists

☐ Parasympathomimetic (miotic) agents, including cholinergic and anticholinesterase agents

☐ Carbonic anhydrase inhibitors (CAIs)

☐ Adrenergic agonists

☐ Hyperosmotic agents

☐ Prostaglandin analogs

The actions and side effects of the various glaucoma medications are listed in Table XI-1 along with dosage information and other concerns (see pp 108–109).

Beta-Adrenergic Antagonists (Beta Blockers)

Five topical beta-adrenergic antagonists are now used for the treatment of glaucoma in the United States: betaxolol, carteolol, levobunolol, metipranolol, and timolol. All except betaxolol are noncardioselective beta$_1$ and beta$_2$ blockers. Beta$_1$ activity is largely cardiac and beta$_2$ activity largely pulmonary. Since betaxolol is a relatively cardioselective beta$_1$-blocking agent, it may be useful in patients with a history of bronchospastic disorders. Carteolol, in addition to producing beta-blocking effects, is claimed to demonstrate intrinsic sympathomimetic activity.

Beta-blocking agents lower IOP by reducing aqueous humor secretion. Beta blockers are additive in combination with miotics and carbonic anhydrase inhibitors. Combinations of beta blockers and adrenergic agonists are generally only slightly additive. The effectiveness of beta blockers may be reduced after prolonged use.

Side effects of beta-adrenergic antagonists are listed in Table XI-1. They include bronchospasm, bradycardia, increased heart block, lowered blood pressure, and reduced exercise tolerance. Diabetic patients may experience reduced glucose tolerance and masking of hypoglycemia signs. Although betaxolol is somewhat less effective than the other beta-adrenergic antagonists in lowering pressure, it may be a safer alternative.

It is important to determine if the patient has ever had asthma prior to the prescription of a beta-blocking agent, which may induce severe bronchospasm in susceptible patients. The pulse should be measured and the beta blocker withheld if the pulse is very slow or if more than first-degree heart block is present. Myasthenia gravis may be aggravated by these drugs.

Other side effects of beta blockers include lethargy, mood changes, depression, altered mentation, light-headedness, syncope, visual disturbances, corneal anesthesia, punctate keratitis, impotence, reduced libido, allergy, and alteration of serum lipids. This change in lipids is less evident in patients using an agent with intrinsic sympathomimetic activity.

Adrenergic Agonists

The adrenergic agonists epinephrine and dipivefrin increase conventional and uveoscleral outflow. Initially, they increase aqueous production. With chronic use, however, they decrease aqueous production. Adding adrenergic agonists to beta antagonists usually produces minimal additional pressure-lowering effects, with rare exceptions. Epinephrine salts used in the treatment of glaucoma include hydrochloride, borate, and bitartrate. Epinephrine bitartrate has about one half the available epinephrine of an equivalent solution of its hydrochloride or borate salt. The borate salt is the least irritating.

Dipivefrin is a pro-drug; it is chemically transformed into epinephrine by esterase enzymes in the cornea. Dipivefrin has greater corneal penetration than epinephrine salts, and the activity of this drug prior to its alteration by the esterase enzymes is relatively low. These qualities give dipivefrin two major advantages over epinephrine salts: A lower topical concentration of dipivefrin has an intraocular effect similar to higher dosages of epinephrine salts. Furthermore, therapeutic effectiveness in the eye can be achieved with fewer topical and systemic side effects.

Table XI-1 lists potential side effects of both epinephrine and dipivefrin. Important systemic side effects include headache, increased blood pressure, tachycardia, arrhythmia, and nervousness. Epinephrine causes adrenochrome deposits from oxidized metabolites in the conjunctiva, cornea, and lacrimal system; and it may stain soft contact lenses (Fig XI-1). The use of these agents often causes pupillary dilation that may precipitate or aggravate angle closure in susceptible patients. Allergic blepharoconjunctivitis occurs in approximately 20% of patients over time. Dipivefrin is tolerated by some patients who are allergic to epinephrine salts. Cystoid macular edema may be precipitated or exacerbated in aphakic and pseudophakic eyes. Since this maculopathy is usually reversible if recognized early, epinephrine or dipivefrin should be used with caution in these eyes. When these drugs are discontinued, rebound conjunctival hyperemia is common. Although this condition is harmless, patients may be disturbed by the appearance and usually need reassurance.

Apraclonidine hydrochloride is an alpha$_2$-adrenergic agonist and clonidine derivative. When administered pre- and postoperatively, the drug is effective in diminishing the acute IOP rise that follows argon laser iridotomy, argon laser trabeculoplasty, Nd:YAG laser capsulotomy, and cataract extraction. Apraclonidine hydrochloride may be effective for the short-term lowering of IOP, but the frequent development of topical sensitivity and tachyphylaxis often limits long-term use. Brimonidine tartrate is also a relatively selective alpha$_2$-adrenergic agonist that may have less tachyphylaxis than apraclonidine in long-term use. Caution must be exercised when using both drugs in patients on monoamine oxidase inhibitor (MAOI) or tricyclic antidepressant therapy and in patients with severe cardiovascular disease. Caution should also be taken when using these drugs concomitantly with beta blockers, antihypertensives, and cardiac glycosides (ophthalmic and systemic). Although effective in acutely lowering IOP in angle-closure glaucoma, these drugs induce vasoconstriction that may prolong iris sphincter ischemia and reduce the efficacy of concurrent miotics.

Parasympathomimetic Agents

Parasympathomimetic agents are divided into two groups: cholinergic agonists are direct-acting, and anticholinesterase agents are indirect-acting. Direct-acting agents

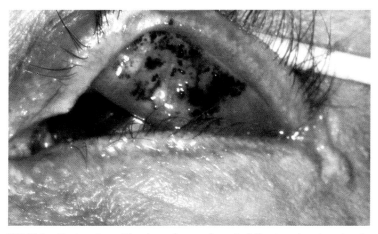

FIG XI-1—Conjunctiva with adrenochrome deposits following chronic epinephrine use.

affect the motor endplates in the same way as acetylcholine. Indirect-acting agents inhibit the enzyme acetylcholinesterase, thereby prolonging and enhancing the action of naturally secreted acetylcholine. Pilocarpine is the most commonly prescribed direct-acting agent. Carbachol has both direct and indirect actions. The indirect-acting agents include echothiophate and demecarium bromide.

Both direct-acting and indirect-acting agents reduce IOP by causing contraction of the ciliary muscle, which pulls the scleral spur to tighten the trabecular meshwork, increasing the outflow of aqueous humor.

The parasympathomimetic agents have been shown to reduce uveoscleral outflow in animals. Theories on their effects on the uveoscleral outflow system in humans are speculative. It is possible that this action may actually worsen the glaucoma if miotics are used in patients with little to no trabecular outflow. In addition, these agents cause the pupillary sphincter to contract (hence their common name, *miotics*), stimulate secretory activity in the lacrimal and salivary glands, and disrupt the blood-aqueous barrier. These actions have little bearing on the IOP-lowering effect of the miotic agents, except in angle-closure glaucoma. Here, the mechanical action of the contracting pupillary sphincter may pull the iris away from the trabecular meshwork.

Miotic agents have been reported to cause retinal detachment in some patients. If possible, an alternate medication may be considered in patients with peripheral retinal disease that predisposes them to retinal detachment.

Induced myopia resulting from ciliary muscle contraction is a side effect that is common to all cholinergic miotic agents. The short-acting drugs may produce varying refractive changes, especially in the young. Brow ache may accompany the ciliary spasm, and the miosis interferes with vision in dim light and in patients with lens opacities.

Sustained-release pilocarpine membranes and pilocarpine gel minimize the pharmacologic side effects of pilocarpine while decreasing the frequency of required

TABLE XI-1. GLAUCOMA MEDICATIONS

CLASS/GENERIC	BRAND NAME	STRENGTH(S)	DOSAGE	HELPFUL IN THESE	CONCERNS	ACTION	SIDE EFFECTS
Beta-adrenergic antagonists (beta blockers)							
Noncardioselective							
● Timolol maleate	Timoptic Timoptic-XE[1] Ocudose[2]	0.25, 0.5%	qd, bid	Young patients; cataract, hypertensive	Asthma, COPD, heart block, mental changes in elderly, altered blood lipid profile	Reduces aqueous secretion	Blurring, irritation, allergy, corneal anesthesia, punctate keratitis, brady-cardia, heart block, bronchospasm, decreased libido, mood changes
○ Timolol hemihydrate	Betimol	5.12 mg/mL	qd, bid	Same as above	Same as above	Same as above	Same as above
● Levobunolol HCl	Betagan	0.25, 0.5%	qd, bid	Same as above	Same as above	Same as above	Same as above
Ⓦ Metipranolol	OptiPranolol	0.3%	qd, bid	Same as above	Same as above	Same as above	Same as above
● Carteolol HCl	Ocupress	1.0%	qd, bid	Same as above	Same as above	Same as above	
Cardioselective							
○ Betaxolol HCl	Betoptic	0.25, 0.5%	qd, bid	Same as above	Same as above, except fewer pulmonary complications	Same as above	Same as above, except fewer pulmonary complications
Adrenergic agonists							
Ⓦ Epinephrine	Epifrin	0.25, 0.5, 1.0, 2.0%	qd, bid	Young patients; cataract	Hypertension, aphakia, soft contact lens; narrow angles	Improves aqueous outflow	Irritation, adrenochrome deposits, allergy, rebound hyperemia, blurred vision, mydriasis, cystoid macular edema in aphakia, hypertension, extra systoles, headache
Ⓦ Epinephrine HCl	Glaucon	1.0, 2.0%	qd, bid				
Ⓦ Epinephryl borate	Epinal	0.5, 1.0, 2.0%	qd, bid				
	Eppy/N	0.5, 1.0, 2.0%	qd, bid				
Ⓦ Epinephrine bitartrate	Epitrate	2.0%	qd, bid				
● Dipivefrin HCl	Propine	0.1%	qd, bid	Patients with systemic epinephrine problems or allergy	Similar to epinephrine	Same as epinephrine	Same as epinephrine, but pro-drug struc-ture makes systemic side effects less likely
Alpha2-adrenergic agonist							
Ⓦ Apraclonidine HCl	Iopidine	1.0% 0.5%	Pre- and postlaser tid, short term	Patients undergoing anterior segment laser	Similar to epinephrine; avoid with severe glaucomatous optic neuropathy, ischemia	Reduces aqueous secretion	Irritation, topical sensitivity, vasovagal attack
● Brimonidine tartrate	Alphagan	0.2%	tid	Less tachyphylaxis than apraclonidine HCl (reported)	Patients receiving monoamine oxidase inhibitor (MAOI) ther-apy. Caution in using concomi-tant drugs such as beta blockers, antihypertensives, and cardiac glycosides (ophthalmic and systemic). Caution in patients taking tricyclic antidepressants, which can affect the metabolism and uptake of amines	Reduces aqueous humor production and increases uveoscleral outflow	Oral dryness, ocular hyperemia, irrita-tion, headache, blurring, foreign body sensation, fatigue, ocular pruritus, photophobia, ocular ache, ocular dry-ness, tearing, upper respiratory symp-toms, eyelid edema, conjunctival edema, dizziness, gastrointestinal symptoms, conjunctival blanching, insomnia, depression, anxiety, syncope
Parasympathomimetic (miotic) agents							
Cholinergic agents							
● Pilocarpine HCl	Isopto Carpine Pilocar	0.25–10.0% 0.5, 1.0, 2.0, 3.0, 4.0, 6.0%	bid to qid bid to qid	Older patients with minimal cataract, aphakes	Central opacity, young patients, peripheral retinal pathology	Improves aqueous outflow	Miosis, decreased night vision, variable induced myopia, brow ache, exacerbation of visual defect of cataract, cataracto-genic (?), induced angle closure, retinal tear or detachment
	Pilopine HS gel	4.0%	qd				
	Ocusert Pilo	20, 40 μg/hr	weekly				Less intense miosis, less variability of myopia
						Same as above	

● Pilocarpine nitrate	Pilagan	1.0, 2.0, 4.0%	bid to qid				
● Carbachol	Isopto Carbachol	0.75, 1.5, 2.25, 3.0%	bid to tid	Same as pilocarpine	Same as pilocarpine	Improves aqueous outflow	Same as pilocarpine, but longer duration reduces variability. Stronger, so miosis, myopia, brow ache may be more intense
Anticholinesterase agents							
● Echothiophate iodide	Phospholine Iodide	0.03, 0.06, 0.125, 0.25%	qd, bid	Aphakic, pseudophakic	General anesthesia, ocular surgery, retinal detachment, cataract	Improves aqueous outflow	Intense miosis, iris pigment epithelial cysts, induced myopia, cataract, retinal detachment, paradoxical angle closure, punctal stenosis, intense bleeding and inflammation with ocular surgery, abdominal cramps, diarrhea, enuresis, prolonged recovery from succinylcholine
Ⓦ Demecarium bromide	Humorsol	0.125, 0.25%	qd, bid				
● Physostigmine	Eserine ointment / Isopto Eserine	0.25% / 0.25, 0.5%	Post-cataract surgery / qd, bid				
Carbonic anhydrase inhibitors							
Systemic							
Acetazolamide	Diamox	125, 250 mg	bid to qid	When topicals fail; acute glaucoma		Reduces aqueous secretion	Lethargy, paresthesias, malaise, abdominal cramps, diarrhea, nausea, anorexia, renal stones, impotence, loss of libido, mental depression, hypokalemia, acidosis, aplastic anemia, thrombocytopenia, agranulocytosis
	Diamox Sequels	500 mg	qd, bid				
	Diamox	500 mg	Usually ≤1g/day				
Acetazolamide parenteral		5–10 mg/kg[3]	q 6–8 h		Lethargy, depression, weight loss, acidosis, renal stones, bone marrow depression		
Dichlorphenamide	Daranide	50 mg	bid, tid				
Methazolamide	Neptazane	25, 50 mg	bid, tid	Same as acetazolamide	Same as acetazolamide	Same as above	Same as above
Topical							
● Brinzolamide	Azopt	1% suspension	tid	Similar to systemic CAIs	Similar to systemic CAIs	Same as above	Same as above
● Dorzolamide	Trusopt	2.0%	tid	Similar to systemic CAIs	Similar to systemic CAIs	Same as above	Same as above
Prostaglandin analogs							
Ⓒ Latanoprost solution	Xalatan	.005%	qd (preferred qhs)	No statistically significant effects on cardiovascular or respiratory system; additional IOP lowering effect when used in combination with timolol, pilocarpine, dipivefrin, and acetazolamide	Long-term effects of increased melanosomes in the eye currently unknown	Enhanced uveoscleral outflow	Increased pigmentation of the iris, conjunctival hyperemia, blurred vision, foreign body sensation, irritation, increased pigmentation of the iris, punctate epithelial keratopathy, hypertrichosis, cystoid macular edema, anterior uveitis
Hyperosmotic agents[4]							
Mannitol parenteral	Osmitrol	5–25% solution	2 g/kg body weight	Very high pressure; acute glaucoma	Congestive heart failure, urinary retention	Reduces vitreous volume	Congestive heart failure, diabetic keto-acidosis (glycerin), headache, subdural and subarachnoid hemorrhages
Glycerin	Osmoglyn	50% solution	4–7 oz	Same as mannitol, less likely to produce congestive heart failure	Worsens diabetes, nausea, vomiting	Same as above	Same as above
Isosorbide	Ismotic	45% solution	4–7 oz	Same as glycerin, safer for diabetics	Diarrhea	Same as above	Same as above

[1]Timoptic-XE is a gel-forming solution recommended for qd dosing. [2]Ocudose is a preservative-free formulation of Timoptic for patients sensitive to benzalkonium chloride. [3]In infants and children. [4]Osmotic agents should not be used chronically or repeatedly. Color designates bottle cap color. Ⓦ = white; Ⓒ = clear/translucent. However, generic products may not follow these color guidelines.

dosing. In the membrane form, a polymer sandwich containing adsorbed pilocarpine (Ocusert) releases medication at a steady rate for approximately 1 week. The induced myopia is more stable, and miosis is less marked than with eyedrop therapy. (See chapter on ocular pharmacology in BCSC Section 2, *Fundamentals and Principles of Ophthalmology.*) Generally, the release of pilocarpine and the induced symptoms are greatest during the first 24 hours. This treatment is tolerated better when administered at bedtime.

In its other sustained-release formulation, pilocarpine adsorbed to a plastic gel is administered once daily at bedtime. Although the IOP-lowering effect may last 24 hours in some patients, other individuals show loss of drug effect after 18–20 hours. Induced myopia and miosis are less prominent with the gel than with drops, but they may still interfere with vision during waking hours. If the gel has not dissipated by morning, the patient may have blurred vision upon awakening. Ocusert and pilocarpine gel may be useful in younger patients, in patients bothered by variable myopia or intense miosis, in older patients with lens opacities, and in people who have difficulty complying with more frequent dosing regimens.

Indirect-acting miotics and the stronger direct-acting agents may induce a paradoxical angle closure, because contraction of the ciliary muscle leads to forward movement of the lens–iris diaphragm, an increase in the anteroposterior diameter of the lens, and a very miotic pupil. These effects may increase pupillary block. In patients with a central opacity such as a posterior subcapsular cataract, the miosis may be visually disabling. However, the concomitant administration of an alpha-adrenergic agonist such as phenylephrine may cause a larger pupil without interfering with the reduction of IOP.

The indirect-acting miotics are cataractogenic, and evidence suggests that the direct-acting agents may be weakly cataractogenic. Indirect-acting miotics may induce generalized cataract formation in addition to anterior subcapsular opacity. They may also induce the formation of iris pigment epithelial cysts. The stronger miotics may cause epiphora by both direct lacrimal stimulation and by punctal stenosis. These agents may also cause ocular surface changes resulting in drug-induced pemphigoid. Reports of increased inflammation following surgery associated with the use of stronger miotics might encourage the surgeon to discontinue these agents prior to surgery. Anticholinesterase agents should be discontinued and other agents substituted at least 2–4 weeks prior to ocular surgery, because they can cause significant bleeding during surgery and severe fibrinous iridocyclitis postoperatively. Because miotic agents can break down the blood-aqueous barrier their use should be limited in treating uveitic glaucomas.

While direct-acting miotics rarely induce systemic side effects, indirect-acting medications may be responsible for systemic parasympathetic stimulation. Diarrhea, abdominal cramps, increased salivation, bronchospasm, and even enuresis may result. Pseudocholinesterase activity in the red blood cells is depressed for 6 weeks after cessation of eyedrops. Since cholinesterase is suppressed throughout the body, depolarizing agents such as succinylcholine should be avoided while the patient is using these eyedrops and for 6 weeks after discontinuation. Because of the potential for significant ocular and systemic side effects, indirect-acting parasympathomimetic agents are used less commonly than direct-acting agents. In fact, indirect-acting agents are usually reserved for treating glaucoma in aphakic and pseudophakic eyes when IOP is not controlled by less toxic agents and in phakic eyes when filtering surgery has failed.

Carbonic Anhydrase Inhibitors (CAIs)

Carbonic anhydrase inhibitors are agents that reduce aqueous formation by direct inhibition of carbonic anhydrase in the ciliary body and, to a lesser extent, by producing a generalized acidosis. These agents are most commonly used orally for chronic and acute glaucoma. In acute situations (e.g., acute angle-closure glaucoma) they can be given orally, intramuscularly, and intravenously. A topical formulation—dorzolamide—is also available. Because of the significant systemic side effects of these drugs, long-term systemic use is reserved for patients whose glaucoma cannot be controlled by alternative topical therapy alone.

Acetazolamide and methazolamide are the agents most commonly used; others in this group include dichlorphenamide, ethoxzolamide, and topical dorzolamide. Methazolamide has a longer duration of action and is less bound to serum protein than is acetazolamide. Methazolamide and sustained-release acetazolamide seem to be the best tolerated of the CAIs.

Side effects of CAI therapy are usually dose-related. Many patients develop paresthesia of the fingers or toes or complain of lassitude, loss of energy, and anorexia. Weight loss is common. Abdominal discomfort, diarrhea, loss of libido, impotence, an unpleasant taste in the mouth, and severe mental depression may also occur. There is a marked increase in formation of calcium oxalate and calcium phosphate renal stones. Because methazolamide has greater hepatic metabolism and causes less acidosis, it may be less likely to cause renal lithiasis than is acetazolamide.

Since CAIs are chemically derived from the sulfa drugs, they have similar allergic reactions and cross-reactivity. Aplastic anemia is a rare but potentially fatal idiosyncratic reaction to CAIs. Thrombocytopenia and agranulocytosis can also occur. Although routine complete blood counts have been suggested, they are not predictive of this idiosyncratic reaction and not routinely recommended. Hypokalemia is a potentially serious complication that is especially likely when a CAI is used concurrently with another drug that causes potassium loss (e.g., a thiazide diuretic). Serum potassium should be monitored regularly in such patients.

Clearly, CAIs are potent medications with significant side effects. The lowest dose that reduces IOP to an acceptable range should be used. Methazolamide is often effective in doses as low as 25–50 mg given two or three times daily. Acetazolamide may be started at 62.5 mg every 6 hours. Higher doses may be used if tolerated. Sustained-release formulations such as Diamox Sequels may have fewer side effects.

Topical CAI compounds also reduce aqueous formation by direct inhibition of carbonic anhydrase in the ciliary body and induce fewer systemic side effects. A number of compounds have been investigated in recent years. Dorzolamide is currently available in a 2% solution for use three times a day. Adverse effects include superficial punctate kerotopathy and systemic side effects similar to those induced by systemic administration, although often less intense. Severe lassitude, a rare but possible effect, may limit the use of this agent.

Prostaglandin Analogs

Latanoprost solution is a prostaglandin analog that appears to lower IOP by enhancing uveoscleral outflow. An advantage of this class of drugs is a once-daily dosing, preferably at bedtime. Other advantages include the lack of cardiopulmonary contraindications and the additivity to other antiglaucoma agents. However, a side effect also unique to this class of drugs is darkening of the iris as a result of an increased number of melanosomes within the melanocytes. Long-term effects are currently unknown.

Hyperosmotic Agents

Common hyperosmotic agents include oral glycerin and isosorbide and intravenous mannitol. Isosorbide is a particularly useful oral agent for diabetic patients because, unlike glycerin, it is not metabolized into sugar. Hyperosmotic agents are used to control acute episodes of elevated IOP. They are rarely administered for longer than a few days because the effects of hyperosmotic agents are transient as a result of the rapid reequilibration of the osmotic gradient. They become less effective over time, and a rebound elevation in IOP may occur if the agent penetrates the eye and reverses the osmotic gradient.

When given systemically, hyperosmotic agents lower IOP by increasing the blood osmolality. The increased blood osmolality creates an osmotic gradient between the blood and the vitreous humor, drawing water from the vitreous cavity and reducing IOP. The larger the dose and more rapid the administration, the greater the reduction in IOP because of the increased gradient. A substance distributed only in extracellular water (e.g., mannitol) is more effective than a drug distributed in total body water (e.g., urea). When the blood-aqueous barrier is disrupted, the osmotic agent enters the eye faster than when the blood-aqueous barrier is intact, thus reducing both the effectiveness of the drug and its duration of action.

Side effects of these drugs include headache, mental confusion, backache, and acute congestive heart failure and myocardial infarction. The rapid increase in extracellular volume and cardiac preload caused by hyperosmotic agents may precipitate or aggravate congestive heart failure. Intravenous administration is more likely than oral dosage to cause this problem. In addition, subdural and subarachnoid hemorrhages have been reported after treatment with hyperosmotic drugs. Glycerin can produce hyperglycemia or even ketoacidosis in diabetic patients, since it is metabolized into sugar and ketone bodies.

General Approach to Medical Treatment

Open-Angle Glaucoma

Characteristics of the medical agents available for treatment of glaucoma are summarized in Table XI-1. The clinician should tailor therapy for open-angle glaucoma to the individual needs of the patient. In general, a target IOP is established as the goal. However, the effectiveness of therapy can only be established by careful repeated scrutiny of the patient's optic nerve and visual field status.

Treatment is usually initiated with a single topical medication, unless the starting IOP is extremely high, in which case combination therapy may be indicated. A beta blocker is commonly the drug of choice for initial therapy, assuming no medical contraindication rules it out. Because of the variability of IOP, it is best (unless the IOP is extremely high) to test the medication in one eye until the effectiveness of therapy has been established. At that point, both eyes can be treated. Compliance and efficacy must be monitored regularly.

Patients should be instructed about how to space their medications. It may be useful to coordinate the administration of medication with a part of the daily routine, such as meals. Drops due at the same time should be separated by at least 5 minutes to prevent washout of the first by the second. Patients should be shown how to administer eyedrops. Nasolacrimal occlusion or gentle eyelid closure reduces the systemic side effects from topical eye medications by decreasing systemic absorption and may enhance the efficacy of some drops. Teaching the patient to close the eyes for 1 full minute after instillation of the drop helps promote corneal penetration and reduce systemic absorption.

If one drug is not adequate to reduce IOP to the estimated desired safe level, another agent should be tried. If no single agent controls the pressure, a combination of topical agents should be used. A beta blocker with a miotic or topical CAI or an adrenergic agonist with a miotic or topical CAI is usually the best combination. Adrenergic antagonists combined with agonists are only occasionally additive. Systemic CAIs may be tried if other agents are not effective or well tolerated.

Patients often do not associate systemic side effects with topical drugs and, consequently, seldom volunteer symptoms. Therefore, the ophthalmologist should inquire about these symptoms. Communication with the primary care physician is important not only to let the family doctor know the potential side effects of antiglaucoma medications but also to discuss the interactions of any other systemic medications with the glaucoma process. Modification of systemic beta-blocker therapy for hypertension, for example, may affect glaucoma control. Physicians should be aware that as the complexity and expense of the medical regimen increase, compliance may decline.

Patients with open-angle glaucoma require careful monitoring. IOP, while important, is only one factor. Optic nerve photographs or drawings and visual fields must be compared periodically to determine the stability of the disease (see chapter VI). The condition of the patient and the severity of the disease determine how often each of these parameters must be checked. If the cupping or visual field damage shows evidence of progression despite apparent control of acceptable IOP, other diseases should be considered (see normal-tension glaucoma, chapter VII). Other possible explanations include an IOP level too high for the particular patient, IOP that may be spiking at times when the patient is not in the office, concomitant angle closure, or poor patient compliance.

Angle-Closure Glaucoma

Medical treatment for acute angle-closure glaucoma is aimed at preparing the patient for laser iridotomy. The goals of medical treatment are to reduce IOP rapidly to prevent further damage to the optic nerve, to clear the cornea, to reduce intraocular inflammation, to allow pupillary constriction, and to prevent formation of posterior and peripheral anterior synechiae (see chapter VIII, Angle-Closure Glaucoma).

Epstein DL, Allingham RR, Schuman JS, eds. *Chandler and Grant's Glaucoma.* 4th ed. Baltimore: Williams & Wilkins; 1997.

Hoskins HD Jr, Kass MA, eds. *Becker-Shaffer's Diagnosis and Therapy of the Glaucomas.* 6th ed. St Louis: CV Mosby Co; 1989.

Moses RA, Hart WM, eds. *Adler's Physiology of the Eye: Clinical Application.* 8th ed. St Louis: CV Mosby Co; 1987.

Ritch R, Shields MB, Krupin T, eds. *The Glaucomas.* vols 1–3. St Louis: CV Mosby Co; 1996.

Tasman W, Jaeger EA, eds. *Duane's Clinical Ophthalmology.* Philadelphia: JB Lippincott Co; 1996.

CHAPTER XII

Surgical Therapy of Glaucoma

Surgical therapy of glaucoma is undertaken when medical therapy is not appropriate, not tolerated, not effective, or not properly utilized by a particular patient. Surgery is usually the primary approach for infantile and pupillary-block glaucoma. In contrast, surgery is usually considered for open-angle glaucoma only when medical therapy has failed. The relative roles of medical and surgical intervention in the therapy of open-angle glaucoma are the subject of ongoing study.

It is important to note that patients with far advanced visual field loss or field loss that is impinging on fixation are at risk for total loss of central acuity following a surgical procedure. The mechanism of this phenomenon is not known, but possibilities include cystoid macular edema, early postoperative IOP spiking, and optic nerve ischemia. Before contemplating a surgical procedure, the ophthalmologist must consider factors such as the patient's general health, presumed life expectancy, and status of the fellow eye.

Patients should be informed of the purpose and expectations of their surgery: to arrest progressive visual loss caused by their glaucoma. Patients should understand that glaucoma surgery alone rarely improves vision and that glaucoma medications may still be required postoperatively, that surgery may fail completely, and that vision could be lost as a result of surgery.

Knowledge of both the internal and external anatomy of the limbal area is essential for successful results, whether incisional or laser surgery is considered. Figure XII-1 illustrates various incisional approaches.

Open-Angle Glaucoma

Surgery is indicated in open-angle glaucoma when IOP cannot be maintained at a level low enough to prevent further damage to the optic nerve. The glaucoma may be uncontrolled for various reasons:

☐ Maximal medical therapy fails to adequately reduce IOP.

☐ The amount of medical therapy necessary to control IOP is not well tolerated or places the patient at unacceptable risk.

☐ Optic nerve cupping or visual field loss is progressing despite apparently normal IOP levels.

☐ The patient cannot comply with the necessary medical regimen.

The roles of laser surgery and incisional surgery are currently in flux. Although, generally, surgery for a patient whose medical regimen cannot satisfactorily control

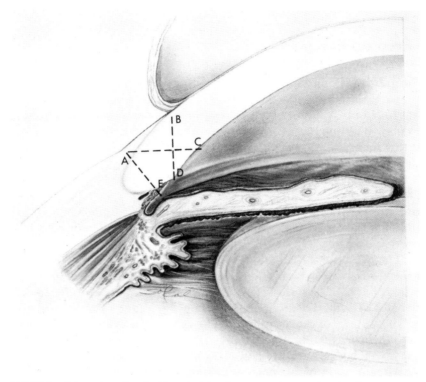

FIG XII-1—Orientation of an incision. Incision lines enter the anterior chamber at various levels, depending on their point of origin and whether they are perpendicular or beveled in relation to the corneal surface. (*A*) Posterior limit of the external corneoscleral sulcus and posterior limit of the limbus. An incision perpendicular to the corneal tissues at this point (*A–E*) enters the anterior chamber at approximately the midpoint of the trabecular meshwork. A beveled incision at this point (*A–C*) enters the chamber anterior at Schwalbe's line. An incision parallel to the visual axis (*B–D*) must begin at the anterior limit of the conjunctival insertion in order to enter the chamber at Schwalbe's line. These relationships should be kept in mind when determining how to enter the anterior chamber from the limbus. In a narrow-angle eye, the internal aspects may be shifted forward so that incision *A–E* might fall into the ciliary body. In congenital glaucomas the anatomical relationships are more variable. (Reproduced by permission from Hoskins HD Jr, Kass MA, eds. *Becker-Shaffer's Diagnosis and Therapy of the Glaucomas.* 6th ed. St Louis: CV Mosby Co; 1989.)

his or her glaucoma begins with a laser trabeculoplasty, alternative laser procedures and incisional surgery may be shown to be more effective. If laser trabeculoplasty fails to bring IOP under control, a trabeculectomy or another filtering procedure (e.g., tube shunt) should be considered.

When an initial filtering procedure is not adequate to control the glaucoma, and a repeat attempt adding medical therapy is not successful, revision surgery, repeat filtering surgery, tube-shunt, and cyclodestructive procedures are indicated.

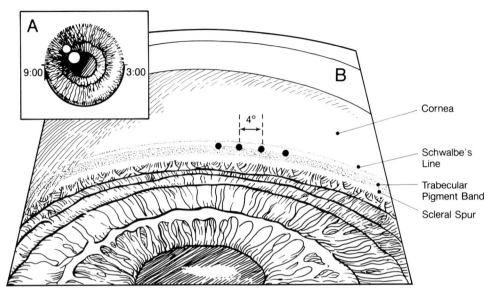

FIG XII-2—*A* and *B*, Position of argon laser trabeculoplasty treatment in the trabecular meshwork. (After Solish AM, Kass MA. Laser trabeculoplasty. In: Waltman SR, Keates RH, Hoyt CS, eds. *Surgery of the Eye*. New York: Churchill Livingstone; 1988:1.)

Laser Surgery

Laser trabeculoplasty (LTP)   In the argon procedure, a 50-μm laser beam of 0.1 second duration is focused through a goniolens on the anterior pigmented edge of the trabecular meshwork (Fig XII-2). Application to the posterior trabecular meshwork tends to produce inflammation, prolonged elevation of IOP, and peripheral anterior synechiae. Although some clinicians use a standard power for all patients, many prefer to adjust the power setting (500–1200 mW) to achieve the desired end point: blanching of the trabecular meshwork or production of a tiny bubble. If a large bubble appears, the power is reduced. The diode procedure is similar; a 75-μm laser beam is focused through a goniolens with a power setting of 600–1000 mW.

The mechanism of action of LTP remains unclear, although outflow facility improves following successful trabeculoplasty. In this procedure as originally described, laser energy was applied to the entire circumference (360°) of the trabecular meshwork. Evidence suggests that many patients have a satisfactory IOP reduction with less risk of short-term pressure elevation when only one half of the circumference (180°) is treated, using approximately 40–50 applications. The adjunctive use of topical apraclonidine may blunt postoperative pressure elevation.

Some surgeons still prefer initial 360° therapy. In either case, short-term postoperative monitoring is of paramount importance. From 4 to 6 weeks should be allowed for the full effect of the first treatment before a decision is made about additional treatment. Approximately 80% of patients with medically uncontrolled open-angle glaucoma experience a drop in IOP for a minimum of 6–12 months following LTP. Longer-term data have shown that 50% of patients with an initial response maintain a significantly lower IOP 3–5 years after treatment. Success at 10 years approximates 30%. Elevation of IOP may recur in some patients after months or even years of control.

Additional laser treatment may be helpful in some patients, especially if the entire angle has not been treated previously. Retreatment of an angle that has been fully treated (approximately 80–100 spots over 360°) has a lower success rate and a higher complication rate than does primary treatment.

Ritch R, Shields MB, Krupin T, eds. *The Glaucomas.* St Louis: CV Mosby; 1996.

Wise JB, Witter SL. Argon laser therapy for open-angle glaucoma: a pilot study. *Arch Ophthalmol.* 1979;97:319–322.

Laser trabeculoplasty effectively reduces IOP in patients with primary open-angle glaucoma, pigmentary glaucoma, and exfoliation syndrome. It works least effectively in patients with inflammatory glaucoma, recessed angles, or membranes in the angle or in young patients who have developmental defects. Aphakic and pseudophakic eyes may respond less favorably than phakic eyes; therefore, LTP is more effective before than after cataract surgery. IOP reduction does not seem to be diminished by subsequent cataract extraction.

The question the surgeon must address is when in the course of glaucoma therapy is it appropriate to employ LTP, since the duration of efficacy appears limited. Laser trabeculoplasty is sometimes considered as the initial therapy for primary open-angle glaucoma and perhaps other open-angle glaucomas as well. The Glaucoma Laser Trial (GLT) Research Group conducted a multicentered, randomized clinical trial to assess the efficacy and safety of LTP as an alternative to treatment with topical medication in patients with newly diagnosed, previously untreated primary open-angle glaucoma. Within the first 2 years of follow-up, LTP as initial therapy appeared to be as effective as medication. However, more than half of eyes treated initially with laser required the addition of one or more medications to control IOP. Many ophthalmologists believe it is premature to recommend LTP as an initial therapy until more long-term data are available. The patient should understand that LTP may postpone the need for conventional surgery or additional medications. However, as with all glaucoma therapy, patients should not assume that their glaucoma is cured by this procedure, and they should be reminded that their disease requires lifelong monitoring.

Glaucoma Laser Trial Research Group. The Glaucoma Laser Trial (GLT). 2. Results of argon laser trabeculoplasty versus topical medicines. *Ophthalmology.* 1990;97:1403–1413.

The most significant complication of laser trabeculoplasty is a transient rise in IOP, which occurs in approximately 20% of patients. IOP may reach 50–60 mm Hg and may cause additional damage to the optic nerve. This rise is less common when only 180° of the angle is treated per session. Such IOP elevations are of particular concern in patients with advanced cupping. Rises in IOP are usually evident within the first 2–4 hours after treatment, and all patients should be monitored closely for this complication. Measures to prevent this post-LTP pressure elevation include the use of topical apraclonidine, additional topical medications, hyperosmotic agents, and ice packs. Apraclonidine should be used with caution in patients with advanced cupping.

Other complications of LTP include the rare persistent elevation of IOP requiring filtering surgery, transient or persistent iridocyclitis, hyphema, and the formation of peripheral anterior synechiae. Histopathologic examination suggests that LTP may stimulate the growth of trabecular meshwork endothelial cells. The long-term implications of this finding remain unknown.

In addition to argon and diode lasers, other laser systems are currently under development for use in laser trabeculoplasty. Critical considerations in selecting the appropriate type of laser are corneal transparency, spot size, and penetration depth.

Panek WC. Role of laser treatment in glaucoma. In: *Focal Points: Clinical Modules for Ophthalmologists*. San Francisco: American Academy of Ophthalmology; 1993;11:1.

Incisional Surgery

Filtering procedures   Filtering surgery is indicated in most glaucoma patients when medical and/or laser treatment have failed to control open-angle glaucoma. It is rarely indicated as primary therapy. The goal of filtering surgery is to create a new pathway for the bulk flow of aqueous humor from the anterior chamber through the sclera into the subconjunctival and sub-Tenon's spaces. Filtering procedures in common usage include guarded and full-thickness techniques.

Trabeculectomy. Trabeculectomy, a guarded, partial-thickness filtering procedure, is performed by removing a block of limbal tissue beneath a scleral flap (Fig XII-3). The scleral flap limits the outflow of aqueous and thereby reduces the complications associated with early hypotony, such as cataract, serous and hemorrhagic choroidal effusion, macular edema, and optic nerve edema. Because of the lower incidence of postoperative complications, trabeculectomy is the most commonly performed filtering operation, although it may not lower IOP as effectively in the long term as would a full-thickness procedure. The use of antifibrotic agents such as mitomycin-C and 5-fluorouracil, combined with techniques of releasable sutures or laser suture lysis, enhances the longevity of guarded procedures.

Full-thickness sclerectomy. Full-thickness filtering operations are performed by removing a block of limbal tissue with a punch, trephine, laser, or cautery (Fig XII-4). The advantage of full-thickness filtering procedures is that they lower IOP and can maintain the lowered level for long periods of time. Historically, ophthalmic surgeons performed these procedures on patients in whom a postoperative IOP lowered to the mid- to high teens would not be considered adequate. Currently, the use of concurrent or subsequent antifibrotic agents such as mitomycin-C or 5-fluorouracil may equalize the outcomes for full-thickness and guarded filtering procedures. The disadvantages of full-thickness compared to partial-thickness techniques include a higher incidence of postoperative flat anterior chamber, cataract, hypotony, and leakage of filtering blebs. As with all surgical procedures, individual preferences evolve with experience.

Combined cataract and filtering surgery. Indications for combining glaucoma surgery (usually trabeculectomy) with cataract extraction include:

☐ Glaucoma that is uncontrollable either medically or after laser trabeculoplasty when visual function is significantly impaired by a cataract

☐ The need for cataract extraction in a glaucoma patient who has advanced visual field loss

A combined procedure may prevent postoperative IOP rise. Success and complication rates are acceptable for trabeculectomy combined with cataract extraction

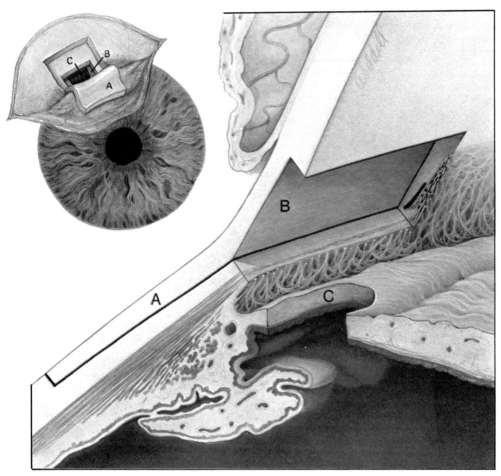

FIG XII-3—Trabeculectomy. Limbus-based or fornix-based conjunctival flap is incised. *A,* A half-thickness scleral flap 3–4 mm wide is dissected into clear cornea. A block excision (1.5 × 2 mm) or a punch excision at area *B,* anterior to scleral spur, may include trabeculum, Schlemm's canal, and peripheral cornea. *C,* A peripheral iridectomy is performed under the excision site. (Reproduced with permission from Kolker AE, Hetherington J, eds. *Becker-Schaffer's Diagnosis and Therapy of the Glaucomas.* 5th ed. St Louis: CV Mosby Co; 1983.)

and posterior chamber intraocular lens implantation. A variety of techniques have proven successful. Combined procedures are generally less effective than filtering procedures alone in controlling IOP over time, although combined procedures using small-incision phacoemulsification techniques with an antifibrotic agent may equal the effectiveness of filtering surgery alone. For patients in whom glaucoma is the greatest immediate threat to vision, filtering surgery alone should be performed

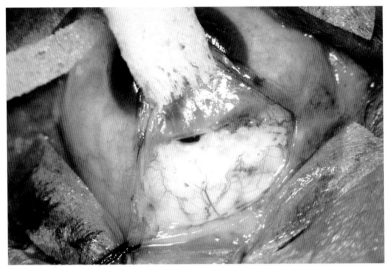

FIG XII-4—Intraoperative photograph of full-thickness sclerectomy performed with Descemet's punch.

first. The postoperative discontinuation of miotics is often enough to increase visual acuity so that cataract extraction and IOL implantation may be delayed.

Hoskins HD Jr, Migliazzo CV. Filtering surgery for glaucoma. In: *Focal Points: Clinical Modules for Ophthalmologists.* San Francisco: American Academy of Ophthalmology; 1986;4:9.

Weinreb RN, Mills RP, eds. *Glaucoma Surgery: Principles and Techniques.* Ophthalmology Monograph 4, 2nd ed. San Francisco: American Academy of Ophthalmology; 1998.

Preoperative considerations in filtering surgery Filtering surgery is less successful in younger or aphakic/pseudophakic patients. A lower success rate is also found in patients with uveitic glaucoma or with previously failed filtration procedures. Black patients have a higher failure rate with filtering surgery.

Control of preoperative inflammation with corticosteroids helps to reduce postoperative iritis and scarring of the filtering bleb. Anticholinesterase agents should be discontinued and replaced temporarily by alternative medications at least 2–3 weeks before surgery to reduce bleeding and iridocyclitis. Replacement of topical adrenergic agonists should also be considered.

Operative considerations in filtering surgery Intraocular pressure should be reduced as close as possible to normal levels before surgery is performed, to minimize the risk of expulsive choroidal hemorrhage. Systemic hypertension should be controlled as well.

To enable the surgeon to control the anterior chamber depth, a paracentesis should be performed. This procedure allows for intraoperative testing of the patency of the filtration site as well as of the integrity of the conjunctival closure.

Minimizing tissue manipulation reduces the risks of bleeding, inflammation, and scarring. The conjunctiva should be handled gently to prevent the creation of a buttonhole. Hemorrhage under a conjunctival flap is undesirable and should be prevented if possible by judicious use of cautery. However, excessive cautery may induce scarring.

A sclerectomy, whether or not it is under a scleral flap, should be anterior enough to provide access to the anterior chamber. A peripheral iridectomy must be sufficiently basal to prevent postoperative occlusion of the sclerectomy by underlying iris; it must also be anterior to the iris root to prevent hemorrhage or damage to the ciliary body. Meticulous closure of the Tenon's and conjunctival incisions either separately or together will help to prevent postoperative leakage with resultant shallowing of the anterior chamber. With adjunct antifibrotic agent use, separate layer closure is recommended.

The intraoperative application of antifibrotic agents such as mitomycin-C results in greater early and midterm success and lower IOP. However, serious postoperative complications may occur.

Postoperative considerations in filtering surgery   Topical cycloplegic agents, antibiotics, and corticosteroids are administered postoperatively. Sub-Tenon's corticosteroids or a short course of systemic corticosteroids may be administered to reduce scarring and inflammation, especially in patients with poor prognoses.

5-fluorouracil inhibits fibroblast proliferation and has proven useful in reducing scarring after filtering surgery. Although it was originally advocated for high-risk groups such as patients with aphakic/pseudophakic eyes, neovascular glaucoma, or a history of previous failed operations, this agent is now injected subconjunctivally on a routine basis by many surgeons. Regimens for administration vary according to the observed healing response. A total of 5 mg in 0.1 cc can be injected with relatively mild discomfort. Complications such as corneal epithelial defects commonly occur and require discontinuation of 5-fluorouracil injections.

Techniques to prevent early postoperative hypotony by allowing tighter wound closure initially include the use of releasable flap suture techniques or the placement of additional sutures that can be cut postoperatively to facilitate outflow following trabeculectomy. In laser suture lysis the conjunctiva is compressed with either a Zeiss goniolens or a Hoskins condensing lens, and the argon laser (set at 300–400 mW, 50 μm, and 0.02–0.1 second) can usually lyse the selected nylon suture with one application. Surgeons commonly wait at least 48 hours before performing laser suture lysis. Filtration is best enhanced if lysis or suture release is completed within 2 weeks, or before the flap has fibrosed. This period is lengthened when antifibrotic agents have been used.

Complications of filtering surgery   Early complications of filtering surgery include infection, hypotony, flat anterior chamber, hyphema, formation or acceleration of cataract, transient IOP elevation, cystoid macular edema, suprachoroidal hemorrhage, persistent uveitis, dellen formation, and loss of vision. Late complications include leakage or failure of the filtering bleb, cataract, and endophthalmitis. The filtering bleb can leak, produce dellen, or expand so as to interfere with eyelid function or extend onto the cornea and interfere with vision. Filtering blebs are dynamic, evolve over time, and must be monitored.

The techniques of choroidal tap and anterior chamber re-formation should be familiar to any surgeon who performs filtering surgery, which incurs the risk of flat chamber associated with choroidal detachment. Suprachoroidal fluid is drained through one or more posterior sclerotomies, as the chamber is deepened through a paracentesis.

The use of contact lenses with a filtering bleb presents special problems. Contact lenses may be difficult to fit in the presence of a filtering bleb, or the lens may ride against the bleb, causing discomfort and increasing the risk of infection.

Other Procedures (Incisional and Nonincisional)

Procedures to control IOP include laser sclerostomy, tube-shunt surgery, ciliary body ablation, and cyclodialysis.

Laser and mechanical sclerostomy   Laser sclerostomy and automated microtrephination have shown potential as alternatives to conventional filtering surgery. Successful laser sclerostomy procedures, both ab externo and ab interno, have been developed using erbium, holmium, excimer, pulsed dye, and continuous wave Nd:YAG lasers. Ab interno sclerostomies have been successfully created using an automated microtrephine. Future clinical trials should clarify the optimum laser technique(s) for creating and maintaining an opening from the anterior chamber to the subconjunctival space.

Tube-shunt surgery   Many different types of devices have been proposed to aid filtration by shunting aqueous to a site posterior to the limbus. Shunts in current use generally have a tube placed in the anterior chamber. In the Molteno implant, the tube is attached to an acrylic plate sutured to the sclera. The Schocket shunt procedure uses an encircling silicone band beneath the rectus muscles. Variations include tube shunts with pressure-sensitive, unidirectional valves such as the Krupin and Ahmed implants.

These devices, and other similar types of implants, are generally reserved for difficult glaucoma cases in which conventional filtering surgery has failed. Rarely, tube-shunt implantation may be a primary procedure in neovascular glaucoma. Success rates have been encouraging, but implant procedures share many of the complications associated with conventional filtering surgery. They also incur unique problems related to the tubes and plates, such as erosion.

Ciliary body ablation procedures   Several surgical procedures reduce aqueous secretion by destroying a portion of the ciliary body. The secretory activity of ciliary body epithelium can be inhibited by treating the ciliary body with cyclocryotherapy, diathermy, therapeutic ultrasound, and thermal lasers, such as continuous wave Nd:YAG, argon, and diode. Each of these procedures may result in prolonged hypotony, pain, inflammation, cystoid macular edema, hemorrhage, and even phthisis bulbi.

Cyclocryotherapy has been the most commonly used of these methods over the past few decades. However, interest has been increasing in *transscleral Nd:YAG* and *transscleral diode laser cyclophotocoagulation;* both appear to cause less pain and inflammation than cyclocryotherapy. Use of the argon laser aimed at the ciliary processes via an endoprobe with or without endoscopic visualization or via a goniolens is possible in only a small percentage of patients, which limits the usefulness of these techniques. Ciliary body ablation is generally reserved for eyes that have been or are likely to be unresponsive to other modes of therapy. Pain following these procedures may be substantial, and patients should be provided with adequate analgesics, including narcotics, during the immediate postoperative period.

Cyclodialysis Cyclodialysis is performed infrequently but may be helpful in aphakic patients who have not responded to filtering surgery. In cyclodialysis a small scleral incision is made approximately 4 mm from the limbus. A fine spatula is passed
under the sclera into the anterior chamber. This spatula disinserts a portion of the
ciliary muscle from the scleral spur and creates a cleft in the angle, providing
direct communication between the anterior chamber and the suprachoroidal space.
Complications include bleeding, inflammation, cataract, and the stripping of
Descemet's membrane. Profound hypotony, or an equally significant rise in IOP
should the cleft close, may also occur.

Angle-Closure Glaucoma

Laser Surgery

Laser iridotomy The treatment of pupillary-block glaucoma, whether primary or
secondary, is a laser iridotomy or an incisional iridectomy (see below). These procedures provide an alternative route for aqueous trapped in the posterior chamber to
enter the anterior chamber, allowing the iris to recede from occluding the trabecular meshwork (Fig XII-5). Laser surgery has become the preferred method in almost

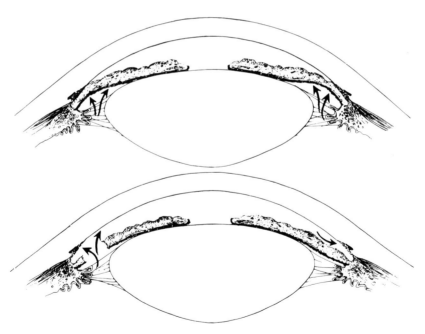

FIG XII-5—Angle-closure glaucoma. Laser iridotomy or surgical iridectomy breaks the
pupillary block and results in opening of the entire peripheral angle if no permanent
peripheral anterior synechiae are present. (Reproduced and modified with permission from
Kolker AE, Hetherington J, eds. *Becker-Shaffer's Diagnosis and Therapy of the Glaucomas.*
5th ed. St Louis: CV Mosby Co; 1983.)

all cases. Both the argon laser and Nd:YAG laser are effective in relieving pupillary block.

The argon laser may be used to produce an iridotomy in most eyes, but very dark and very light irides present technical difficulties. Using a condensing contact lens, the typical initial laser settings are 0.02–0.1 second of duration, 50-μm spot size, and 800–1000 mW of power. There are a number of variations in technique; iris color dictates which technique is chosen. Complications include localized lens opacity, acute rise in IOP (which may damage the optic nerve), transient or persistent iritis, early closure of the iridotomy, and corneal and retinal burns.

The Q-switched Nd:YAG laser generally requires fewer pulses and less energy than an argon laser to create a patent iridotomy. Also, the effectiveness of this laser is not affected by iris color. With a condensing contact lens, the typical initial laser setting is 2–5 mJ. Potential complications include corneal burns, disruption of the anterior lens capsule or corneal endothelium, bleeding (usually transient), postoperative IOP spike, inflammation, and delayed closure of the iridotomy. To prevent damage to the lens the surgeon must use caution with the Q-switched Nd:YAG laser in performing further enlargement of the opening once patency is established.

Ritch R, Shields MB, Krupin T, eds. *The Glaucomas.* St Louis: CV Mosby; 1996.

Shields MB. *Textbook of Glaucoma.* 3rd ed. Baltimore: Williams & Wilkins; 1992: 448–452.

Laser gonioplasty   Gonioplasty is a technique to deepen the angle that is rarely useful in angle-closure glaucoma. Stromal burns are created with the argon laser in the peripheral iris to cause contraction and flattening. Typical laser settings are 0.2 second duration, 200-μm spot size, and 200–300 mW of power. This procedure can be used to open the angle temporarily, in anticipation of a more definitive iridotomy or iridectomy, or in other types of angle closure such as plateau iris syndrome and nanophthalmos.

Lasers for ciliary-block glaucoma   Both the argon and Q-switched Nd:YAG lasers may be useful in treating ciliary-block glaucoma. If ciliary processes are visible, they can be shrunk with direct application of the argon laser. The Nd:YAG laser can rupture the anterior hyaloid face with as little as 0.5 mJ of energy.

Goniophotocoagulation   Argon laser goniophotocoagulation, in conjunction with panretinal photocoagulation, may delay impending angle closure from anterior segment neovascularization. The thermal laser beam is aimed to close new vessels where they cross the scleral spur. Although adequate panretinal photocoagulation represents the definitive treatment, in rare cases goniophotocoagulation may be an adjunctive therapy.

Filtering surgery may be indicated following panretinal photocoagulation if iris neovascularization has abated, IOP remains uncontrolled with medical therapy, and visual potential remains good.

Goniophotodisruption   Peripheral anterior synechiae that have formed following angle closure or in ICE syndrome may be disrupted with the Q-switched Nd:YAG laser focused through a goniolens.

Selective laser trabecular ablation   By selective uptake by the trabecular meshwork of dye, the trabecular meshwork can be targeted by a wavelength-matched laser to ablate only this tissue, resulting in lowered IOP.

Laser ciliary body ablation   Ciliary body ablation can be accomplished in chronic angle-closure glaucoma with the continuous wave Nd:YAG laser and the argon laser to reduce aqueous secretion (see p 122).

Incisional Surgery

Peripheral iridectomy   Incisional surgical iridectomy may be required if a patent iridotomy cannot be achieved with a laser. Such situations include a cloudy cornea, a flat anterior chamber, and insufficient patient cooperation.

Cataract extraction   When pupillary block is associated with a visually significant cataract, lens extraction might be considered as a primary procedure. However, laser iridotomy may stop an acute attack of pupillary block, so that cataract surgery may be performed more safely at a later time.

Chamber deepening and goniosynechialysis   When peripheral anterior synechiae develop in cases of angle-closure glaucoma, iridectomy alone may not relieve the glaucoma adequately. Chamber deepening through a paracentesis with intraoperative gonioscopy may break PAS of relatively recent onset. A viscoelastic agent and/or cyclodialysis spatula may be useful, in a procedure known as *goniosynechialysis,* to break synechiae.

> Campbell DG, Vela A. Modern goniosynechialysis for the treatment of synechial angle-closure glaucoma. *Ophthalmology.* 1984;91:1052–1060.

Vitrectomy for ciliary-block glaucoma   Ciliary-block glaucoma may require incisional surgery when medical and/or laser treatments fail. A stab incision into the vitreous 3 mm posterior to the limbus will disrupt the anterior hyaloid face and enable vitreous aspiration or core vitrectomy. Care must be taken to avoid the lens in phakic patients.

Filtration and tube-shunt surgery   As with open-angle glaucoma, filtration and tube-shunt surgery may be required in angle-closure glaucoma to control IOP.

Childhood Glaucoma

Incisional Surgery

Goniotomy and trabeculotomy   The procedures of choice in the surgical treatment of primary infantile glaucoma are goniotomy and trabeculotomy. With a *goniotomy,* a needle-knife is passed across the anterior chamber, and a superficial incision is made in the anterior aspect of the trabecular meshwork under gonioscopic control (Fig XII-6). A clear cornea is necessary to provide an adequate view of the chamber angle.

In a *trabeculotomy,* a fine wirelike forked instrument (trabeculotome) is inserted into Schlemm's canal from an external incision, and the trabecular meshwork is torn by rotating the trabeculotome into the anterior chamber (Fig XII-7). Tra-

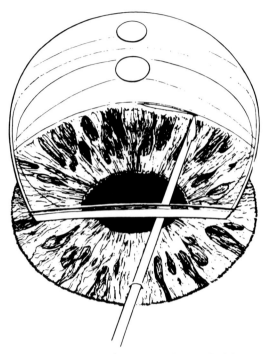

FIG XII-6—Drawing showing goniotomy incision as seen through a surgical contact lens. (Reproduced with permission from Shaffer RN. *Am J Ophthalmol.* 1966; 62:613–618. Copyright by the Ophthalmic Publishing Company.)

beculotomy is particularly useful if the cornea is too cloudy to allow adequate visualization for goniotomy. However, the abnormal angle anatomy associated with congenital glaucomas sometimes precludes localization of Schlemm's canal.

Complications of both of these operations include hyphema, infection, lens damage, and uveitis. Descemet's membrane may be stripped during trabeculotomy. Serious complications in children often result from the general anesthesia required. Because of anesthetic risks, bilateral procedures are indicated in some children.

Filtering surgery with antifibrotic agents (see p 118) and tube-shunt surgery (see p 122) represent other types of incisional surgery that may be successful in cases of childhood glaucoma.

Laser Surgery

Trabeculopuncture may be performed with variable success in younger patients using the Q-switched Nd:YAG laser and a contact goniolens. Energy as high as 10 mJ with multiple applications may be necessary to achieve an opening into Schlemm's canal. Lesser energy may be adequate to disrupt trabecular meshwork bands in juvenile glaucomas.

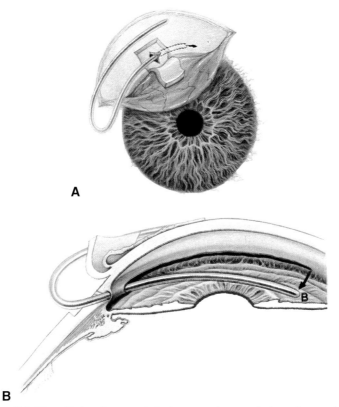

FIG XII-7—Trabeculotomy. *A*, Probe is gently passed along the canal with little resistance for 6–10 mm. *B*, By rotating the probe internally, the surgeon ruptures the trabeculum, and the probe appears in the anterior chamber with minimum bleeding. (Reproduced and modified with permission from Kolker AE, Hetherington J, eds. *Becker-Shaffer's Diagnosis and Therapy of the Glaucomas.* 5th ed. St Louis: CV Mosby Co; 1983.)

Ciliary body ablation with transscleral continuous wave Nd:YAG or diode laser cyclophotocoagulation (see p 122) may be useful in cases of childhood glaucoma refractory to other treatments but may also cause scleral thinning.

Minckler DS, Van Buskirk EM, eds. Glaucoma. In Wright KW, ed. *Color Atlas of Ophthalmic Surgery.* Philadelphia: JB Lippincott Co; 1992.

Thomas JV, Belcher CD III, Simmons RJ, eds. *Glaucoma Surgery.* St Louis: Mosby–Year Book; 1992.

Weinreb RN, Mills RP, eds. *Glaucoma Surgery: Principles and Techniques.* Ophthalmology Monograph 4, 2nd ed. San Francisco: American Academy of Ophthalmology; 1998.

CHAPTER XIII

Low-Vision Aids in Glaucoma Patients

Chronic severe advanced glaucoma characteristically results not only in constriction of the peripheral visual field but in loss of central retinal sensitivity as well. Low vision implies a level of visual function that prevents an individual from performing visual tasks with standard optical correction of his or her refractive error. The patient with low vision from glaucoma may benefit from the use of various devices:

☐ Optical systems of contact lenses

☐ Telescopes

☐ Large-print computers

☐ Closed-circuit television systems

These and other low-vision aids may enhance the patient's visual performance by magnification of the object or image of interest.

Evaluation of Low-Vision Patients with Glaucoma

As part of the evaluation of the low-vision patient, a concise, detailed history is very important in prescribing or recommending visual aids. In addition to the particular ocular condition, the evaluation must also consider the medical and social history of the individual. A detailed analysis of the specific activities that the patient finds difficult and an awareness of what the patient hopes most to gain by low-vision aids is essential. This analysis will help minimize the frequent "drawerful" of low-vision lenses and the like, which may be of no use to a particular patient.

Disorders of the peripheral visual field such as glaucoma may leave macular function relatively intact but still limit a patient's mobility. When central vision is affected in addition to the peripheral visual field, the functional visual loss can become a significant handicap. Patients with advanced glaucoma are often aware of some generalized dimming of vision, as well as peripheral visual loss. They may also notice a loss of contrast. Many of these patients can benefit from merely modifying their visual tasks to focus on situations that allow high contrast and by using good lighting.

Management

Refraction is of paramount importance to provide the best possible correction of the macular function if it is still intact. Some individuals may also benefit from yellow-tinted lenses, which may enhance contrast. The clinician should also be careful that visual acuity testing include the small optotypes on the Snellen visual acuity chart to be sure that the patient is not merely reading a letter that is larger than that patient's intact, but constricted, central field. If the central visual field is less than 10° and the Snellen acuity is less than 20/60, a magnified image may not be useful or appreciated because a large portion may have to extend beyond the borders of the remaining field. Telescopic magnification is seldom useful and the least amount of magnification that the patient subjectively finds helpful should be prescribed.

The most useful prescribed aids for these patients are handheld magnifiers in the range of 4–12 diopters, yellow-tinted lenses, and closed-circuit television (CCTV) products. The use of CCTV with a zoom lens for electronic magnification is especially helpful for reading and writing, because it offers greater viewing distance and does not require the patient to hold a lens, thus freeing both hands. Any viewing distance can be used, and the degree of magnification may be altered by use of the zoom lens or by the individual's moving closer to the television screen. In addition, some patients can improve the contrast or reverse the polarity and have light letters on a dark background to help compensate for some loss in contrast sensitivity.

Recent advances in computer technology may provide great benefit through voice-output computers as well as other voice-activated electronic devices or computers. Newer software allows the individual to scan the written page in accompaniment to the voice output. Finally, patients with advanced peripheral field defects as well as limitation of central acuity may benefit from referral to an agency for the visually impaired. Special training in mobility may be offered to the patient, as well as instruction for the patient's friends and family. Often the patient with advanced glaucoma and limited central vision is the most difficult subject for rehabilitation, but many still benefit from some very simple types of assistance.

See also BCSC Section 3, *Optics, Refraction, and Contact Lenses.*

Fletcher DC, ed. *Low Vision Rehabilitation: Caring for the Whole Person.* Ophthalmology Monograph 12. San Francisco: American Academy of Ophthalmology; 1999.

BASIC TEXTS

Glaucoma

Anderson DR. *Automated Static Perimetry.* St Louis: Mosby–Year Book; 1992.

Drance SM, Anderson DR, eds. *Automatic Perimetry in Glaucoma: A Practical Guide.* Orlando, FL: Grune & Stratton; 1985.

Epstein DL, Allingham RR, Schuman JS, eds. *Chandler and Grant's Glaucoma.* 4th ed. Baltimore: Williams & Wilkins; 1997.

Harrington DO. *The Visual Fields: A Textbook and Atlas of Clinical Perimetry.* 6th ed. St Louis: CV Mosby Co; 1989.

Higginbotham EJ, Lee DA, eds. *Management of Difficult Glaucoma: A Clinician's Guide.* London: Blackwell Scientific Publications; 1994.

Hoskins HD Jr, Kass MA, eds. *Becker-Shaffer's Diagnosis and Therapy of the Glaucomas.* 6th ed. St Louis: CV Mosby Co; 1989.

Minckler DS, Van Buskirk EM, eds. Glaucoma. In: Wright KW, ed. *Color Atlas of Ophthalmic Surgery.* Philadelphia: JB Lippincott Co; 1992.

Moses RA, Hart WM, eds. *Adler's Physiology of the Eye: Clinical Application.* 8th ed. St Louis: CV Mosby Co; 1987.

Ritch R, Shields MB, Krupin T, eds. *The Glaucomas.* St Louis: CV Mosby Co; 1996.

Shields MB. *Textbook of Glaucoma.* 3rd ed. Baltimore: Williams & Wilkins; 1992.

Tasman W, Jaeger EA, eds. *Duane's Clinical Ophthalmology.* Philadelphia: JB Lippincott Co; 1996.

Thomas JV, Belcher CD III, Simmons RJ, eds. *Glaucoma Surgery.* St Louis: Mosby–Year Book; 1992.

RELATED ACADEMY MATERIALS

Focal Points: Clinical Modules for Ophthalmologists

Balyeat HD. Cataract surgery in the glaucoma patient, part 1: a cataract surgeon's perspective (Module 3, 1998).

Beck AD, Lynch MG. Pediatric glaucoma (Module 5, 1997).

Camras CB. Diagnosis and management of complications of glaucoma filtering surgery (Module 3, 1994).

Drake MV. A primer on automated perimetry (Module 8, 1993).

Gross RL. Cyclodestructive procedures for glaucoma (Module 4, 1992).

Heuer D, Lloyd MA. Management of glaucomas with poor surgical prognoses (Module 1, 1995).

Hodapp EA, Anderson DR. Treatment of early glaucoma (Module 4, 1986).

Jampel HD. Normal (low) tension glaucoma (Module 12, 1991).

Lieberman MF. Glaucoma and automated perimetry (Module 9, 1993).

Liebmann JM. Pigmentary glaucoma: new insights (Module 2, 1998).

Lynch MC, Brown RH. Systemic side effects of glaucoma therapy (Module 4, 1990).

McGrath DJ, Ferguson JG Jr., Sanborn GE. Neovascular glaucoma (Module 7, 1997).

Miller KN, Carlson AN, Foulks GN, et al. Associated glaucoma and corneal disorders (Module 4, 1989).

Panek WC. Role of laser treatment in glaucoma (Module 1, 1993).

Quigley HA. Nerve fiber layer assessment in managing glaucoma (Module 5, 1988).

Ritch R. Exfoliation syndrome (Module 9, 1994).

Rockwood EJ. Medical treatment of open-angle glaucoma (Module 10, 1993).

Samples JR. Management of glaucoma secondary to uveitis (Module 5, 1995).

Schwartz B. Optic disc evaluation in glaucoma (Module 12, 1990).

Skuta GL. Cataract surgery in the glaucoma patient, part 2: a glaucoma surgeon's perspective (Module 4, 1998).

Walton DS. Childhood glaucoma (Module 10, 1990).

Wand M. Diagnosis and management of angle-closure glaucoma (Module 10, 1988).

Wilensky JT. Diagnosis and treatment of pigmentary glaucoma (Module 9, 1987).

Publications

Lane SS, Skuta GL, eds. *ProVision: Preferred Responses in Ophthalmology.* Series 3 (Self-Assessment Program, 1999).

Skuta GL, ed. *ProVision: Preferred Responses in Ophthalmology.* Series 2 (Self-Assessment Program, 1996).

Walsh TJ, ed. *Visual Fields: Examination and Interpretation* (Ophthalmology Monograph 3, 2nd ed, 1996).

Weinreb RN, Mills RP, eds. *Glaucoma Surgery: Principles and Techniques* (Ophthalmology Monograph 4, 2nd ed, 1998).

Wilson FM II, ed. *Practical Ophthalmology: A Manual for Beginning Residents* (1996).

Slide-Script

Coleman A. *Glaucoma: Diagnosis and Management* (Eye Care Skills for the Primary Care Physician Series, 1994).

Fong DS. *Eye Care for the Elderly* (Eye Care Skills for the Primary Care Physician Series, 1999).

Multimedia

ProVision Interactive: Clinical Case Studies. (Volume 2: Retina and Glaucoma on CD-ROM, 1997).

Continuing Ophthalmic Video Education

Cohn HC. *Interactive Gonioscopy: A "Test Yourself" Video;* and Mandal AK, Naduvilath TJ. *Microsurgical Techniques and Results of Combined Trabeculotomy-Trabeculectomy for Developmental Glaucoma* (1998).

Fellman RL. *Molteno Implant Surgery* (1989).

Lewis RA. *Goldmann Applanation Tonometry* (1988).

Minckler DS. *Angle-Closure Glaucoma* (1989).

Sherwood MB. *Management of High-Risk Glaucoma* (1994).

Van Buskirk EM. *Glaucoma Filtration Surgery: Trabeculectomy and Variations* (1988).

Wilson RP. *Management of Combined Cataract and Glaucoma* (1989).

Preferred Practice Patterns

Preferred Practice Patterns Committee, Glaucoma Panel. *Primary Open-Angle Glaucoma Suspect* (1995).

Preferred Practice Patterns Committee, Glaucoma Panel. *Primary Angle-Closure Glaucoma* (1996).

Preferred Practice Patterns Committee, Glaucoma Panel. *Primary Open-Angle Glaucoma* (1996).

Ophthalmic Procedures Assessments

Ophthalmic Procedures Assessment Committee. *Laser Peripheral Iridotomy for Pupillary-Block Glaucoma* (1994).

Ophthalmic Procedures Assessment Committee: *Laser Trabeculoplasty for Primary Open-Angle Glaucoma* (1996).

LEO Clinical Topic Updates

Brandt J. *Glaucoma* (1995).

To order any of these materials, please call the Academy's Customer Service number at (415) 561-8540.

CREDIT REPORTING FORM

BASIC AND CLINICAL SCIENCE COURSE
Section 10

1999–2000

CME Accreditation

The American Academy of Ophthalmology is accredited by the Accreditation Council for Continuing Medical Education to sponsor continuing medical education for physicians.

The American Academy of Ophthalmology designates this educational activity for a maximum of 20 hours in category 1 credit toward the AMA Physician's Recognition Award. Each physician should claim only those hours of credit that he/she has actually spent in the educational activity.

If you wish to claim continuing medical education credit for your study of this section, you must complete and return the study question answer sheet on the back of this page, along with the following signed statement, to the Academy office. This form must be received within 3 years of the date of purchase.

I hereby certify that I have spent _____ (up to 20) hours of study on the curriculum of this section, and that I have completed the study questions. (The Academy, *upon request,* will send you a transcript of the credits listed on this form.)

☐ *Please send credit verification now.*

Signature _____
                                                                                    Date

Name:_____

Address: _____

City and State:_____ Zip: _____

Telephone: (_____) _____ *Academy Member ID# _____
                    area code

*   *Your ID number is located following your name on any Academy mailing label and on your Monthly Statement of Account.*

Section Evaluation

Please indicate your response to the statements listed below by placing the appropriate number to the left of each statement.

1 = agree strongly
2 = agree
3 = no opinion
4 = disagree
5 = disagree
   strongly

_____ This section covers topics in enough depth and detail.

_____ This section's illustrations are of sufficient number and quality.

_____ The references included in the text provide an appropriate amount of additional reading.

_____ The study questions at the end of the book are useful.

In addition, please attach a separate sheet of paper to this form if you wish to elaborate on any of the statements above or to comment on other aspects of this book.

Please return completed form to: **American Academy of Ophthalmology**
P.O. Box 7424
San Francisco, CA 94120-7424
ATTN: Clinical Education Division

SECTION COMPLETION FORM

BASIC AND CLINICAL SCIENCE COURSE

ANSWER SHEET FOR SECTION 10

Question	Answer	Question	Answer
1	a b c d	15	a b c d
2	a b c d e	16	a b c d
3	a b c d	17	a b c d e
4	a b c d e	18	a b c d
5	a b c d e	19	a b c d
6	a b c d	20	a b c d e
7	a b c d	21	a b c d e
8	a b c d e	22	a b c d e
9	a b c d	23	a b c d e
10	a b c d e	24	a b c d e
11	a b c d e	25	a b c d e f
12	a b c d	26	a b c d e
13	a b c d e	27	a b c d
14	a b c d e		

STUDY QUESTIONS

STUDY QUESTIONS

1. In the physiology of aqueous humor formation, the process that is energy-dependent and independent of the intraocular pressure is

   a. Ultrafiltration
   b. Active transport
   c. Simple diffusion
   d. Bulk flow

2. The prevalence of glaucoma is

   a. Equal in blacks and whites
   b. Two times more common in whites than in blacks
   c. Eight to ten times more common in whites than in blacks
   d. Three to six times higher in blacks than in whites
   e. Two times higher in blacks than in whites

3. The blood-aqueous barrier function of the ciliary body is

   a. Related to tight junctions within the pigmented epithelium as a result of cellular membrane permeability restrictions
   b. Related to tight junctions between the apexes of nonpigmented epithelial cells
   c. Related to the integrity and lack of permeability of the vascular elements within the ciliary body
   d. The reason the aqueous and blood concentration of ascorbate are the same

4. The following statements about static threshold perimetry are all true *except*

   a. It allows high-quality perimetry to be performed by perimetrists who have not undergone extensive training.
   b. It is easy for the patient.
   c. The results depend on the size and luminance of the stimulus.
   d. The data can be summarized and analyzed using statistical programs.
   e. The results need to be interpreted in light of the patient's overall clinical picture.

5. The drawing shows a Zeiss gonioprism on the patient's right eye. The clock hour of *angle* that corresponds to the X is

   a. 11:00
   b. 1:00
   c. 4:00
   d. 7:00
   e. 6:00

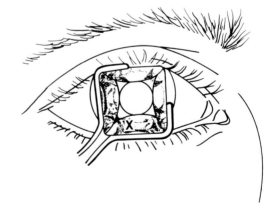

6. The following all characterize normal vessels in the angle *except*

    a. They frequently branch out over the trabecular meshwork in the inter-palpebral space.
    b. They are radial.
    c. They may run circumferentially around the periphery and be visible in only part of the angle.
    d. They originate from the iris, ciliary body, and anterior ciliary arteries.

7. Elevated IOP (≥22 mm Hg) is

    a. Commonly caused by alcohol consumption, particularly in individuals who are not regular consumers of alcohol
    b. Caused in part by defective autoregulation of the peripapillary capillaries
    c. A risk factor for the development of glaucoma
    d. All of the above

8. The Goldmann applanation tonometer

    a. Is of little value in individuals with >5D of corneal astigmatism
    b. Is not affected by alteration in scleral rigidity or by corneal thickness
    c. Displaces approximately 50 µl of fluid from the anterior chamber
    d. Is the most valid and reliable of currently available applanation devices
    e. All of the above

9. All of the following statements regarding Goldmann applanation tonometry are true *except*

    a. The diameter of the applanation tip is 3.06 mm.
    b. The tear film creates surface tension that increases the force of applanation.
    c. The cornea tends to resist deformation, which tends to balance out the surface tension effect of the tear film.
    d. The IOP tends to be overestimated in eyes with low scleral rigidity.

10. Which of the following visual field defects is most characteristic of glaucoma?

    a. Bitemporal hemianopia
    b. Paracentral scotoma
    c. Central scotoma
    d. Superior quadrant anopia
    e. Inferior quandrant anopia

11. Each of the following conditions may produce nerve fiber bundle visual field defects similar to those seen in glaucoma *except*

    a. Chronic papilledema
    b. Optic disc drusen
    c. AION
    d. Occipital infarction
    e. Branch retinal artery occlusion

12. In normal-tension glaucoma

    a. The facility of outflow is significantly reduced
    b. The age of onset of the disease is generally earlier than for primary open-angle glaucoma
    c. Inferotemporal notching of the neuroretinal rim of the optic disc is a common finding at diagnosis
    d. Family history is usually noncontributory for glaucoma

13. The following are histologic changes in glaucoma *except*

    a. Posterior bowing of the lamina cribrosa
    b. Thinning of the retinal nerve fiber layer
    c. Loss of the outer nuclear layer of the retina
    d. Loss of ganglion cells in the retina
    e. Peripapillary atrophy of the choroid

14. Secondary angle closure with pupillary block is the usual mechanism for glaucoma in each of the following *except*

    a. An intumescent lens
    b. Iris neovascularization
    c. Microspherophakia
    d. Uveitis
    e. Ectopia lentis

15. The iridocorneal endothelial (ICE) syndromes include all of the following *except*

    a. Chandler syndrome
    b. Axenfeld-Rieger syndrome
    c. Iris nevus syndrome
    d. Essential iris atrophy

16. A patient with nanophthalmos presents with angle-closure glaucoma. Your attempts at laser peripheral iridotomy are unsuccessful. Your next procedure should be

    a. Trabeculectomy
    b. Phaco—combined
    c. Surgical peripheral iridectomy
    d. Argon laser gonioplasty or iridoplasty

17. Ciliary-block glaucoma, or malignant glaucoma, is associated with all of the following *except*

    a. Responds to aqueous suppressant and hyperosmotic medical management in approximately 50% of cases
    b. Secondary posterior misdirection of aqueous into the vitreous cavity occurs
    c. Occurs only after incisional surgery and never following laser treatment
    d. Occurs most commonly in eyes with a history of angle-closure glaucoma
    e. May occur in aphakic or pseudophakic eyes

18. Which of the following causes of developmental glaucoma does not involve trabeculodysgenesis as a part of its pathophysiology?

    a. Sturge-Weber
    b. Homocystinuria
    c. Aniridia
    d. Peters anomaly

19. Which of the following statements about primary congenital glaucoma is false?

    a. 80% of cases are diagnosed by 1 year of age.
    b. 70%–75% of cases are bilateral.
    c. Most inherited cases are autosomal dominant.
    d. 65% of patients are male.

20. Which of the following beta blockers demonstrates the relative selectivity in the manner described?

    a. Betaxolol: relatively selective for beta$_2$ receptors
    b. Timolol: relatively selective for beta$_1$ receptors
    c. Levobunolol: relatively selective for beta$_2$ receptors
    d. Betaxolol: relatively selective for beta$_1$ receptors
    e. Levobunolol: relatively selective for beta$_1$ receptors

21. The following statements concerning pilocarpine are true *except*

    a. By relaxing tension on the zonular fibers, it may cause narrowing of the anterior chamber.
    b. It is a direct cholinergic agonist.
    c. It reduces IOP by increasing aqueous outflow.
    d. It inhibits acetylcholinesterase.
    e. It is relatively contraindicated in the treatment of uveitic glaucoma.

22. The following statements regarding the topical carbonic anhydrase inhibitor dorzolamide are true *except*

    a. It lowers IOP by decreasing aqueous production.
    b. Difficulties with ocular penetration prolonged the development of this compound.
    c. It has the potential for side effects similar to those of systemic carbonic anhydrase inhibitors, though less frequent.
    d. It has been shown to be clinically effective for once-daily administration.
    e. It may cause Stevens-Johnson syndrome.

23. The agent most likely to be associated with follicular conjunctivitis is

    a. Carbachol
    b. Betaxolol
    c. Dipivefrin
    d. Dorzolamide
    e. Timolol

24. When performing argon laser trabeculoplasty, the most appropriate laser settings are

    a. 200-μm spot size, 0.2-sec duration, 600-mW power
    b. 50-μm spot size, 0.1-sec duration, 800-mW power
    c. 100-μm spot size, 0.5-sec duration, 1500-mW power
    d. 50-μm spot size, 0.1-sec duration, 1500-mW power
    e. 100-μm spot size, 0.1-sec duration, 800-mW power

25. The following complications have been associated with the use of antifibrotic agents as adjuncts to filtering surgery *except*

    a. Corneal vascularization
    b. Endophthalmitis
    c. Hypotony maculopathy
    d. Conjunctival wound leaks
    e. Scleral melting
    f. Corneal ulceration

26. The following are risk factors for delayed suprochoroidal hemorrhage following glaucoma filtering surgery *except*

    a. Aphakia
    b. Advanced age
    c. Systemic hypertension
    d. Hypotony
    e. Hyperopia

27. Following glaucoma filtering surgery, the patient presents on the first postoperative visit with a flat, shallow anterior chamber, a low-lying filtering bleb, and elevated IOP of 40 mm Hg. Possible diagnoses include all of the following *except*

    a. Suprachoroidal hemorrhage
    b. Pupillary block
    c. Ciliochoroidal effusions
    d. Aqueous misdirection

ANSWERS

1. Answer—b. Active transport consumes energy and moves substances against an electrochemical gradient. This process is pressure-independent.

2. Answer—d. The prevalence of glaucoma in the black population is estimated to be three to six times higher than in the white population. In addition, the disease tends to occur at an earlier age in the black population and more commonly results in blindness.

3. Answer—b. The tight junctional barrier between the apexes of nonpigmented epithelial cells presents a selective barrier, which allows diffusion of water and small molecules into the posterior chamber and therefore makes up the blood-aqueous barrier.

4. Answer—b. Most patients find static threshold perimetry fatiguing and unpleasant. It requires an extended period of concentration. Nevertheless, it is extremely valuable.

5. Answer—a. The Zeiss gonioprism mirrors are flat and do not reverse left for right. The superior angle is seen in the inferior mirror, but the nasal and temporal orientation is not changed.

6. Answer—a. Vessels that branch out over the trabecular meshwork are not normal. The two most commonly associated conditions with vessels branching over the trabecular meshwork are diabetes with proliferative retinopathy and central retinal vein occlusion.

7. Answer—c. Alcohol transiently decreases IOP, and the peripapillary capillaries have no known effect on IOP. The possibility of capillary autoregulation is an area of current research.

8. Answer—d. Goldmann applanation tonometry is valid in patients with high corneal astigmatism, but the technique must be modified. Alterations in scleral rigidity and corneal thickness do affect readings. Only 0.5 µl of fluid is displaced by Goldmann tonometry.

9. Answer—d. The IOP in eyes with low scleral rigidity may be underestimated with applanation tonometry, although this effect is more pronounced when techniques of indentation tonometry are used.

10. Answer—b. Choices a, d, and e are neurologic defects. A central scotoma is not typical of glaucoma.

11. Answer—d. All of the above except occipital infarction may produce nerve fiber bundle defects, which can mimic the visual field loss seen in glaucoma. Occipital infarction would typically produce a homonymous hemianopia.

12. Answer—c. The temporal and inferotemporal neuroretinal rim are most affected early in normal-tension glaucoma, although other patterns of disc damage may also be observed.

13. Answer—c. Loss of the outer nuclear layer is not observed in glaucoma. Glaucoma results in loss of ganglion cells and their axons, which make up the retinal nerve fiber layer.

14. Answer—b. All of these conditions are associated with pupillary block except iris neovascularization, which usually causes glaucoma initially by an open-angle mechanism and later by peripheral anterior synechiae.

15. Answer—b. Iris nevus syndrome, Chandler syndrome, and essential iris atrophy are the three characteristic syndromes that relate to the spectrum of findings that may be seen in the iridocorneal endothelial syndromes. Axenfeld-Rieger syndrome is a disorder of the iris stroma that may have other associated ocular and systemic abnormalities.

16. Answer—d. Intraocular surgery in nanophthalmic eyes is fraught with complications, including choroidal effusions and nonrhegmatogenous retinal detachment. Argon laser gonioplasty should be attempted if peripheral iridotomy is unsuccessful.

17. Answer—c. Ciliary-block, or malignant, glaucoma is characterized by a shallow anterior chamber with elevated IOP as a result of posterior misdirection of aqueous. It occurs most commonly following intraocular surgery in eyes with a history of angle-closure glaucoma but may also follow laser iridotomy or other procedures. It has been reported in aphakic and pseudophakic eyes as well as phakic eyes.

18. Answer—b. Trabeculodysgenesis is probably the most common pathophysiologic mechanism behind the entire category of developmental glaucomas. It has never been reported in homocystinuria.

19. Answer—c. Most of the inherited cases (only 10% of all cases) are autosomal recessive.

20. Answer—d. Because of its relative beta$_1$ selectivity, betaxolol has fewer pulmonary side effects. Timolol and levobunolol are nonselective beta blockers.

21. Answer—d. An indirect cholinergic agonist would inhibit cholinesterase. Pilocarpine is a direct-acting cholinergic agonist.

22. Answer—d. Dorzolamide has been approved for three-times-daily dosing.

23. Answer—c. Any topical agent can potentially produce either allergic or toxic surface reaction. However, dipivefrin, a prodrug of epinephrine, is the agent most likely to be associated with follicular conjunctivitis. The incidence of the reaction appears to be lower than with other epinephrine compounds.

24. Answer—b. A 50-µm spot size of 0.1-sec duration is preferred for laser trabeculoplasty. Initial power settings are usually between 600 and 800 mW and then adjusted as necessary to obtain a blanch or occasional small bubble formation in the meshwork.

25. Answer—a. Corneal epithelial defects, wound leaks, bacterial or sterile corneal ulceration, endophthalmitis, hypotony, corneal keratinization, and corneal verticillata are among the conditions reported to be associated with the use of antifibrotic agents.

26. Answer—e. Risk factors generally known to be associated with suprachoroidal hemorrhage include aphakia, hypotony, inflammation, advanced age, previous vitrectomy, myopia, elevated episcleral venous pressure, and long-standing glaucoma.

27. Answer—c. Ciliochoroidal effusions generally present with a low filtering bleb and low IOP as a result of poor aqueous production.

INDEX

Accidental injury, open-angle glaucoma and, 77–80

Acetazolamide, for glaucoma, 109*t*, 111

Active transport, in aqueous humor formation, 14

Acute primary angle-closure glaucoma, 83–84

Adrenergic agonists, for glaucoma, 106, 108*t*

Ahmed implant, for open-angle glaucoma, 122

Air-puff (noncontact) tonometer, 22
  infection control and, 24

Alpha$_2$-adrenergic agonists, for glaucoma, 80, 106, 108*t*

Alpha-adrenergic blockers, angle-closure risk minimized by, 86

Alphagan. *See* Brimonidine tartrate

Angle closure
  gonioscopic identification of, 29–31
  mechanisms and pathophysiology of, 81–82, 81*t*
  provocative tests for, 85–86

Angle-closure glaucoma, 81–95
  acute, 83–84
  chronic, 85
  ciliary-block, 93
    laser therapy for, 124
    vitrectomy for, 125
  classification of, 11, 12*i*, 13*t*
  epithelial downgrowth and, 94
  fibrous downgrowth and, 94
  flat anterior chamber and, 89–90
  Fuchs corneal endothelial dystrophy and, 95
  incisional surgery for, 125
  inflammation causing, 93
  in iridocorneal endothelial syndrome, 91, 92*i*
  laser surgery for, 123–125
  lens-induced, 88–89
  mechanisms of, 81–82, 81*t*
  nanophthalmos and, 95
  neovascular, 90–91
  previous pupillary block and, 89
  primary
    with pupillary block, 82–86
      epidemiology of, 82–83
      pathophysiology of, 83
    without pupillary block, 86, 87*i*, 88*i*
  provocative tests in, 85–86
  retinal surgery and, 94–95
  retinal vascular disease and, 94–95
  retinopathy of prematurity and, 95
  secondary
    with pupillary block, 88–89
    without pupillary block, 89–95
  subacute, 84
  trauma causing, 94
  treatment of
    medical, 113
    surgical, 123–125. *See also specific procedure*
  tumors causing, 91

Angle recession, posttraumatic, 33, 37*i*, 77, 78

Anterior chamber
  deepening, for angle-closure glaucoma, 125
  evaluation of in glaucoma, 26
  flat, angle-closure glaucoma and, 89–90

Anterior chamber angle
  blood vessels in, 33, 35*i*
  evaluation of in glaucoma, 27–36, 37*i*. *See also* Gonioscopy
  gonioscopy landmarks in, 29, 31*i*
  measurement of width of, 29–31
  neovascularization of, angle-closure glaucoma and, 90–91
  trauma affecting, 33, 37*i*, 77, 78

Anterior chamber intraocular lenses, pupillary block and, 88–89

Anterior chamber re-formation, filtering surgery and, 121–122

Anterior synechiae
  chamber angle vessels in formation of, 33
  iris processes differentiated from, 33, 35*i*

Anterior uveal cysts, angle-closure glaucoma caused by, 91

Anticholinesterase agents, for glaucoma, 106–110, 109*t*

Antiglaucoma agents, 105–112. *See also specific type*

Aphakia, pupillary block and, 88

Applanation tonometry, 19–22

Apraclonidine, for glaucoma, 106, 108*t*

Aqueous humor, 14
  formation of, 14–16, 15*i*
  intraocular pressure and, 14–24
  outflow of, 16–17
    tonography for measurement of, 17
    trabecular, 16, 17*i*
    uveoscleral, 16

Aqueous misdirection. *See* Ciliary-block glaucoma

Arcuate Bjerrum scotoma, in glaucoma, 47, 49*i*

Argon laser surgery
  for ciliary ablation, for open-angle glaucoma, 122
  iridotomy, for angle-closure glaucoma, 124
  trabeculoplasty, for open-angle glaucoma, 116–117, 116*i*

Armaly-Drance screening perimetry, 53–54, 53*i*

Arthro-ophthalmopathy, hereditary progressive (Stickler syndrome), childhood glaucoma and, 102*t*

Automated static perimetry, 55
  artifacts seen on, 58–60
  high false-positive rate in, 60, 61*i*
  incorrect corrective lens used in, 60
  learning effect and, 60, 62*i*

Beta-adrenergic antagonists (beta blockers)
  aqueous formation affected by, 14–15
  for glaucoma, 105, 108*t*
    in children, 100
  side effects of, 105, 108*t*

Betagan. *See* Levobunolol

Betaxolol, for glaucoma, 105, 108*t*

Betimol. *See* Timolol

Betoptic. *See* Betaxolol

Biomicroscopy
  in glaucoma, 26
  ultrasound
    in glaucoma, 26, 27*i*
    for plateau iris identification, 86, 87*i*

Bjerrum scotoma, arcuate, in glaucoma, 47, 49*i*

Blepharospasm, in infantile glaucoma, 98

Blindness, glaucoma causing, 9

Blood pressure
  intraocular pressure and, 68
  open-angle glaucoma and, 68

Blue/yellow perimetry, 46

Blunt trauma
  anterior chamber injury caused by, 33, 37*i*, 77, 78
  open-angle glaucoma and, 77, 78

Brimonidine tartrate, 106, 109*t*

Broad thumb syndrome (Rubinstein-Taybi syndrome), childhood glaucoma and, 102*t*

Buphthalmos, in childhood glaucoma, 97, 98

CAIs. *See* Carbonic anhydrase inhibitors

Capsulotomy, posterior, pupillary block after, 89

Carbachol, for glaucoma, 107, 109*t*

Carbonic anhydrase inhibitors
  aqueous formation affected by, 14–15, 111
  for glaucoma, 109*t*, 111
    in children, 100
  side effects of, 109*t*, 111

Cardiovascular disease, open-angle glaucoma associated with, 68

Carteolol, for glaucoma, 105, 108*t*

Cataract, perimetry results affected by, 60

Cataract surgery
  in angle-closure glaucoma, 125
  filtering surgery combined with, 118–120
  flat anterior chamber after, angle-closure glaucoma and, 89–90
  pupillary block after, 89

CCTV. *See* Closed-circuit television

Central retinal vein occlusion
  angle-closure glaucoma and, 95
  open-angle glaucoma and, 68

Cerebrohepatorenal syndrome (Zellweger syndrome), childhood glaucoma and, 102*t*

Chalcosis, open-angle glaucoma and, 78

Chamber deepening, for angle-closure glaucoma, 125

Chandler syndrome, 91, 92*i*
Childhood glaucoma (congenital/infantile
    glaucoma), 97–101, 102–103*t*
  anomalies associated with, 101,
    102–103*t*
  classification of, 13*t*, 97
  clinical features of, 98–99
  cupping in, 40, 98–99
  definition of, 97
  differential diagnosis of, 99, 100*t*
  epidemiology and genetics of, 97
  long-term prognosis and follow-up
    in, 100
  pathophysiology of, 99
  surgery for, 125–127
Cholinergic agents
  for acute angle closure, 84
  for glaucoma, 106–110, 108–109*t*
Choroidal tap, filtering surgery and,
    121–122
Ciliary artery, short posterior branches of
    in optic nerve, 36, 39*i*
Ciliary-block glaucoma (malignant
    glaucoma), 93
  laser therapy for, 124
  vitrectomy for, 125
Ciliary body ablation
  for angle-closure glaucoma, laser, 125
  for childhood glaucoma, 127
  for open-angle glaucoma, 122
Ciliary processes, aqueous humor formed
    by, 14, 15*i*
Closed-circuit television, in low-vision
    management in glaucoma
    patients, 129
Cloverleaf field, 58–60, 59*i*
Cockayne syndrome, childhood glaucoma
    and, 103*t*
Cogan-Reese syndrome (iris nevus
    syndrome), 91, 92*i*
Combined-mechanism glaucoma, 96
  classification of, 13*t*
Compression gonioscopy (indentation/
    pressure gonioscopy), 29, 30*i*, 32*i*
Congenital glaucoma. *See* Childhood
    glaucoma
Conjunctiva, evaluation of in glaucoma,
    26
Contact lenses, with filtering bleb, 122
Contrast sensitivity testing, 46

Cornea, evaluation of in glaucoma, 26
Corneal dystrophy, Fuchs, angle-closure
    glaucoma and, 95
Corrected loss variance, 57
Corrected pattern standard deviation, 57
Corticosteroids, intraocular pressure
    affected by, 80
Cranial nerve II. *See* Optic nerve
CRVO. *See* Central retinal vein occlusion
Cup, optic disc, 41. *See also* Cupping
Cup/disc ratio, 41
Cupping
  glaucomatous, 38–40, 41–42
    elevated intraocular pressure in, 40
    in infants and children, 40, 98–99
    physiologic cupping differentiated
      from, 41–42
  physiologic, glaucomatous cupping
    differentiated from, 41–42
Cyclocryotherapy, for ciliary body
    ablation, for open-angle glaucoma,
    122
Cyclodialysis
  gonioscopic appearance of, 36
  for open-angle glaucoma, 123
Cyclodialysis cleft, open-angle glaucoma
    and, 78
Cyclophotocoagulation, for ciliary body
    ablation
  for childhood glaucoma, 127
  for open-angle glaucoma, 122
Cycloplegics, intraocular pressure affected
    by, 80

Daranide. *See* Dichlorphenamide
Decibel, in perimetry, definition of, 47
Demecarium, for glaucoma, 109*t*
Depression, in perimetry, definition of, 47
Developmental glaucoma, 101, 102–103*t*.
    See also Childhood glaucoma
Diabetes mellitus, open-angle glaucoma
    associated with, 68
Diamox. *See* Acetazolamide
Diapirazole, angle-closure risk minimized
    by, 86
Dichlorphenamide, for glaucoma,
    109*t*, 111
Digital pressure estimation of intraocular
    pressure, 23

Diode laser transscleral cyclophotocoagulation, for ciliary body ablation
for childhood glaucoma, 127
for open-angle glaucoma, 122
Dipivefrin
for glaucoma, 106, 108*t*
side effects of, 106, 108*t*
Diurnal variations, in intraocular pressure, 19
Dorzolamide, for glaucoma, 109*t*, 111
Down syndrome (trisomy 21/trisomy G syndrome), childhood glaucoma and, 102*t*
Drug-induced glaucoma, 80
acute angle-closure, 86
Dyscephalic mandibulo-oculofacial syndrome (Hallermann-Streiff syndrome/François dyscephalic syndrome), childhood glaucoma and, 102*t*

Echothiophate, for glaucoma, 109*t*
Edwards syndrome (trisomy 18/trisomy E syndrome), childhood glaucoma and, 102*t*
Electroretinography, in glaucoma identification, 46
Elevated intraocular pressure
in glaucoma, 7, 19
in glaucoma suspect, 68, 69
in glaucomatous cupping, 40
in pigmentary glaucoma, 75
in primary open-angle glaucoma, 67
after surgery, 79–80
Epifrin. *See* Epinephrine
Epinal. *See* Epinephryl
Epinephrine
for glaucoma, 106, 108*t*
side effects of, 106, 108*t*
Epinephryl, for glaucoma, 108*t*
Epiphora, in infantile glaucoma, 98
Episclera, evaluation of in glaucoma, 26
Episcleral venous pressure, 18
raised, glaucoma and, 77
Epithelial downgrowth, angle-closure glaucoma and, 94
Epitrate. *See* Epinephrine
Eppy/N. *See* Epinephryl
ERG. *See* Electroretinography
Eserine. *See* Physostigmine
Ethoxzolamide, for glaucoma, 111

Exfoliation syndrome, 72–74
open-angle glaucoma and, 74
Extracapsular cataract extraction. *See* Cataract surgery

Fetal alcohol syndrome, childhood glaucoma and, 103*t*
Fibrous downgrowth, angle-closure glaucoma and, 94
Field indices, for threshold perimetry, 57–58
Filtering surgery. *See also specific procedure*
for angle-closure glaucoma, 125
cataract surgery combined with, 118–120
for open-angle glaucoma, 118–122
complications of, 121–122
operative considerations in, 120–121
postoperative considerations in, 121
preoperative considerations in, 120
Flat anterior chamber, angle-closure glaucoma and, 89–90
Flicker sensitivity testing, 46
Fluorophotometry, aqueous formation measured by, 16
Focal ischemia, in normal- (low-) tension glaucoma, 70
Foreign body, metallic intraocular, open-angle glaucoma and, 78
François dyscephalic syndrome (Hallermann-Streiff/dyscephalic mandibulo-oculofacial syndrome), childhood glaucoma and, 102*t*
Fuchs corneal endothelial dystrophy, angle-closure glaucoma and, 95
Fuchs heterochromic iridocyclitis, 77
chamber angle vessels in, 33
glaucoma and, 77
Full-thickness sclerectomy, for open-angle glaucoma, 118, 120*i*
Fundus, evaluation of in glaucoma, 26

Ghost cell glaucoma, 79
Glaucoma. *See also* Angle-closure glaucoma; Open-angle glaucoma
childhood (congenital/infantile), 97–101, 102–103*t*
anomalies associated with, 101, 102–103*t*

classification of, 13*t*, 97
clinical features of, 98–99
cupping in, 40, 98–99
definition of, 97
differential diagnosis of, 99, 100*t*
epidemiology and genetics of, 97
long-term prognosis and follow-up
   in, 100
pathophysiology of, 99
surgery for, 125–127
ciliary-block (malignant), 93
  laser therapy for, 124
  vitrectomy for, 125
classification of, 11–13
clinical evaluation of, 25–65. *See also*
   specific test
  gonioscopy in, 27–36
  history and general examination in,
   25–26, 27*i*
  optic nerve evaluation in, 36–43
  visual field evaluation in, 44–65
combined-mechanism, 96
  classification of, 13*t*
definition of, 7–8
development of, 5–6
developmental, 101, 102–103*t*
ghost cell, 79
hemolytic, 79
hereditary and genetic factors in, 10
history in, 25
juvenile, 97
  genetic basis of, 66
lens-induced
  angle-closure, 88–89
  open-angle, 76
lens particle, 76
low-vision aids in patients with,
   128–129
malignant. *See* Glaucoma, ciliary-block
management of
  medical, 104–113
   agents used in, 105–112. *See also*
    specific type
   general approach to, 112–113
  surgical, 114–127. *See also specific*
   procedure
neovascular, 90–91
normal- (low-) tension, 69–72
  clinical features of, 70
  diagnostic evaluation of, 71–72

differential diagnosis of, 70–71, 71*t*
  prognosis and therapy for, 72
ophthalmoscopic signs of, 41, 41*t*
phacolytic, 76
phacomorphic, 88
primary
  angle-closure
   with pupillary block, 82–86
   without pupillary block, 86, 87*i*, 88*i*
  definition of, 8
  open-angle, 66–68
secondary
  angle-closure
   with pupillary block, 88–89
   without pupillary block, 89–95
  definition of, 8
  open-angle, 72–80
social and economic aspects of, 9
Glaucoma suspect, 68–69
Glaucomatocyclitic crisis
  (Posner-Schlossman syndrome), 77
Glaucomatous cupping, 38–40, 41–42
  elevated intraocular pressure in, 40
  in infants and children, 40, 98–99
  physiologic cupping differentiated from,
   41–42
Glaucon. *See* Epinephrine
Glaukomflecken, in acute primary angle-
  closure glaucoma, 83
Glycerin, for glaucoma, 109*t*, 111–112
Goldmann applanation tonometry, 20–22
  infection control and, 24
Goldmann equation, 14
Goldmann goniolens, 28*i*, 29
Goldmann perimeter, Armaly-Drance
  screening technique using, 53, 53*i*
Goniolens, 28–29, 28*i*
Goniophotocoagulation, laser, for angle-
  closure glaucoma, 124
Goniophotodisruption, laser, for angle-
  closure glaucoma, 124
Gonioplasty, laser, for angle-closure
  glaucoma, 124
Gonioscopy
  approach to, 31*t*
  in children, 98
  direct, 27, 28*i*
  in glaucoma, 27–36, 37*i*
  grading systems for, 32–33, 34*i*

indentation (pressure/compression), 29, 30*i*, 32*i*
  indirect, 28–29, 28*i*
  normal angle landmarks and, 29, 31*i*
Goniosynechialysis, for angle-closure glaucoma, 125
Goniotomy, for childhood glaucoma, 100, 125–126, 126*i*

Haab's striae, in childhood glaucoma, 98
Hallermann-Streiff syndrome (dyscephalic mandibulo-oculofacial syndrome/ François dyscephalic syndrome), childhood glaucoma and, 102*t*
Hemolytic glaucoma, 79
Hemorrhages, splinter, in glaucoma, 43
Hereditary progressive arthro-ophthal-mopathy (Stickler syndrome), childhood glaucoma and, 102*t*
Hruby lens, with slit lamp, for optic disc evaluation, 40
Humorsol. *See* Demecarium
Humphrey pattern standard deviation index, 57
Humphrey STATPAC 2 program, 58, 60
Hyperosmotic agents
  for glaucoma, 109*t*, 112
  side effects of, 112
Hypertension
  ocular, in glaucoma suspect, 68
  systemic, open-angle glaucoma and, 68
Hyphema, open-angle glaucoma and, 78–79

ICE syndrome. *See* Iridocorneal endothelial syndrome
Imbert-Fick principle, in tonometry, 20
Incisional approaches, for glaucoma surgery, 115*i*
Indentation gonioscopy (pressure/compression gonioscopy), 29, 30*i*, 32*i*
Indentation tonometry (Schiøtz tonometry), 19, 22–23
  infection control and, 24
Infantile glaucoma. *See* Childhood glaucoma
Inflammation, ocular
  secondary angle-closure glaucoma and, 93
  secondary open-angle glaucoma and, 76–77

Intraocular foreign body, metallic, open-angle glaucoma and, 78
Intraocular lenses, anterior chamber, pupillary block and, 88–89
Intraocular pressure, 18–24
  aqueous humor dynamics and, 14–24
  digital pressure for estimation of, 23
  distribution of in population, 18–19
  diurnal variations in, 19
  elevated/increased. *See* Elevated intraocular pressure
  factors determining, 7, 7*i*, 19
  in glaucoma suspect, 68, 69
  measurement of, 19–24. *See also* Tonometry
  in infants, 98
Intraocular tumors
  angle-closure glaucoma caused by, 91
  open-angle glaucoma caused by, 76
IOP. *See* Intraocular pressure
Iopidine. *See* Apraclonidine
Iridectomy
  for acute angle closure, 84
  for angle-closure glaucoma, 84, 125
  for elevated intraocular pressure in hyphema, 79
  for plateau iris, 86
Iridocorneal endothelial syndrome, glaucoma in, 91
Iridocyclitis
  Fuchs heterochromic, 77
    chamber angle vessels in, 33
    glaucoma and, 77
  secondary open-angle glaucoma and, 76
Iridoplasty, laser, for plateau iris syndrome, 86, 88*i*
Iridotomy, laser
  for angle-closure glaucoma, 84, 85, 123–124, 123*i*
  for pigmentary glaucoma, 75
Iris
  evaluation of in glaucoma, 26
  neovascularization of, angle-closure glaucoma and, 90–91
  plateau, 86, 87*i*
  posterior bowing of, in pigmentary glaucoma, 75
  progressive atrophy of, 91, 92*i*
Iris bombé, angle-closure glaucoma and, 88

Iris nevus syndrome (Cogan-Reese syndrome), 91, 92*i*

Iris processes, peripheral anterior synechiae differentiated from, 33, 35*i*

Iritis, secondary open-angle glaucoma and, 76–77

Ismotic. *See* Isosorbide

Isopter, definition of, 47

Isopto Carbachol. *See* Carbachol

Isopto Carpine. *See* Pilocarpine

Isopto Eserine. *See* Physostigmine

Isosorbide, for glaucoma, 109*t*, 111–112

Juvenile glaucoma, 97. *See also* Childhood glaucoma
  genetic basis of, 66

Keratitis, angle-closure glaucoma caused by, 93

Kinetic perimetry
  in Armaly-Drance screening, 53
  definition of, 46

Koeppe lens, for gonioscopy, 27, 28*i*

Krukenberg spindles, in pigment dispersion syndrome, 74, 75

Krupin implant, for open-angle glaucoma, 122

Laminar layer (lamina cribrosa) of optic nerve head, 36–38, 39*i*

Laser ciliary body ablation
  for angle-closure glaucoma, 125
  for childhood glaucoma, 127

Laser goniophotocoagulation, for angle-closure glaucoma, 124

Laser goniophotodisruption, for angle-closure glaucoma, 124

Laser gonioplasty, for angle-closure glaucoma, 124

Laser iridoplasty, for plateau iris syndrome, 86, 88*i*

Laser iridotomy
  for acute angle closure, 84
  for angle-closure glaucoma, 84, 85, 123–124, 123*i*
  for pigmentary glaucoma, 75

Laser sclerostomy, for open-angle glaucoma, 122

Laser surgery. *See also specific type*
  for angle-closure glaucoma, 123–125
  for childhood glaucoma, 126–127
  for open-angle glaucoma, 116–118

Laser trabecular ablation, selective, for angle-closure glaucoma, 125

Laser trabeculoplasty, for open-angle glaucoma, 116–118

Laser trabeculopuncture, for childhood glaucoma, 126

Latanoprost solution, 108*t*, 111

Learning effect, in automated perimetry, 60, 62*i*

Lens, evaluation of in glaucoma, 26

Lens-induced glaucoma
  angle-closure, 88–89
  open-angle, 76

Lens particle glaucoma, 76

Lens rim artifact, 58, 59*i*

Levobunolol, for glaucoma, 105, 108*t*

Loss variance index, 57

Low-tension glaucoma. *See* Normal- (low-) tension glaucoma

Low-vision aids, 128–129
  management of, 129
  patient evaluation and, 128

Lowe syndrome (oculocerebrorenal syndrome), childhood glaucoma and, 102*t*

LTP. *See* Laser trabeculoplasty

M cells (magnocellular cells), 36

Magnifiers, handheld, in low-vision management in glaucoma patients, 129

Magnocellular cells (M cells), 36

Malignant glaucoma (ciliary-block glaucoma), 93
  laser therapy for, 124
  vitrectomy for, 125

Mandibulo-oculofacial syndrome, dyscephalic (Hallermann- Streiff syndrome/François dyscephalic syndrome), childhood glaucoma and, 102*t*

Mannitol, for glaucoma, 109*t*, 111–112

Medications, glaucoma caused by. *See* Drug-induced glaucoma

Melanomas, uveal, angle-closure
    glaucoma caused by, 91
Metallic foreign body, intraocular, open-
    angle glaucoma and, 78
Methazolamide, for glaucoma, 109*t*, 111
Metipranolol, for glaucoma, 105, 108*t*
Meyer-Schwickerath and Weyers syndrome
    (oculodentidigital dysplasia),
    childhood glaucoma and, 102*t*
Microspherophakia, pupillary block and
    angle-closure glaucoma caused by, 88
Miosis, perimetry results affected by,
    60, 64*i*
Miotic agents
    angle-closure glaucoma induced by,
      85–86
    for glaucoma, 107–110, 108–109*t*
    in children, 100
Molteno implant, for open-angle
    glaucoma, 122
Moxisylyte
    angle-closure risk minimized by, 86
    in glaucoma diagnosis, 86
Mydriatic agents, angle-closure glaucoma
    induced by, 85
Myopia, open-angle glaucoma associated
    with, 67–68

Na⁺/K⁺ pump, in aqueous outflow, 15
Nanophthalmos, angle-closure glaucoma
    and, 95
Nasal step, in glaucoma, 47, 50*i*
Nd:YAG laser surgery
    ciliary body ablation
      for angle-closure glaucoma, 125
      for childhood glaucoma, 127
      for open-angle glaucoma, 122
    goniophotodisruption, for angle-closure
      glaucoma, 124
    iridotomy, for angle-closure glaucoma,
      124
    trabeculopuncture, for childhood
      glaucoma, 126
Neovascular glaucoma, 90–91
Neptazane. *See* Methazolamide
Nerve fiber bundle defect, 43, 44*i*, 47
Nerve fiber layer of optic nerve head,
    36, 39*i*
Neural rim of optic disc, 41
    recording findings in, 44

Noncontact (air-puff) tonometer, 22
    infection control and, 24
Nonrhegmatogenous retinal detachment,
    elevated intraocular pressure caused
    by, 89
Normal- (low-) tension glaucoma, 69–72
    clinical features of, 70
    diagnostic evaluation of, 71–72
    differential diagnosis of, 70–71, 71*t*
    prognosis and therapy for, 72

Octopus Delta program, 60
Octopus loss variance index, 57
Ocudose. *See* Timolol
Ocular inflammation
    secondary angle-closure glaucoma
      and, 93
    secondary open-angle glaucoma and,
      76–77
Oculocerebrorenal syndrome (Lowe
    syndrome), childhood glaucoma
    and, 102*t*
Oculodentodigital dysplasia (Meyer-
    Schwickerath and Weyers syndrome),
    childhood glaucoma and, 102*t*
Ocupress. *See* Carteolol
Ocusert. *See* Pilocarpine
Open-angle glaucoma, 66–80
    classification of, 11, 12*t*
    filtering procedures for, 118–122
    incisional surgery for, 118–122
    laser surgery for, 116–118
    primary, 66–68
      clinical features of, 67
      disorders associated with, 67–68
      epidemiology of, 66
      hereditary and genetic factors in,
        10, 66
    secondary, 72–80
      accidental injury and, 77–80
      drug use and, 80
      episcleral venous pressure increase
        and, 77
      exfoliation syndrome
        (pseudoexfoliation) and, 72–74
      intraocular tumors causing, 76
      lens-induced, 76
      ocular inflammation and, 76–77

pigmentary, 74–75, 74*i*, 75
    surgical trauma causing, 77–80
  treatment of
    medical, 112–113
    surgical, 114–123. *See also specific procedure*
Ophthalmoscopy, for optic nerve head evaluation, 40
Optic atrophy, glaucomatous, 43, 44*i*
Optic disc. *See also* Optic nerve head
  clinical evaluation of, 41–43, 44*i*
    grading of, 44
    image analysis systems for, 43
  cup of, 41. *See also* Cupping
  examination of, 40
Optic disc hemorrhage, in glaucoma, 43
Optic nerve (cranial nerve II). *See also* Optic nerve head
  anatomy and pathology of, 36–40
  in glaucoma, 36–44
    recording of findings and, 44
    theories of damage and, 40
Optic nerve head. *See also* Optic disc; Optic nerve
  anatomy and pathology of, 36–40
  blood supply of, 36, 39*i*
    autoregulation disturbances in glaucoma and, 40
  clinical evaluation of, 41–43, 44*i*
  divisions of, 36–38, 39*i*
  examination of, 40
  laminar layer of, 36–38, 39*i*
  nerve fiber layer of, 36, 39*i*
  prelaminar layer of, 36, 39*i*
  retinal nerve fiber distribution in, 36, 38*i*
  retrolaminar layer of, 36, 39*i*
Optic neuropathy, in glaucoma, 7
  early changes of, 41, 41*t*
OptiPranolol. *See* Metipranolol
Osmitrol. *See* Mannitol
Osmoglyn. *See* Glycerin

P cells (parvocellular cells), 36
Panretinal photocoagulation, acute angle-closure glaucoma after, 95
Paracentesis, in filtering surgery, 120
Paracentral scotoma, in glaucoma, 47, 48*i*
Parasympathomimetic agents, for glaucoma, 106–110, 108–109*t*

Pars plana vitreous surgery, acute angle-closure glaucoma after, 94
Parvocellular cells (P cells), 36
Patau syndrome (trisomy 13), childhood glaucoma and, 102*t*
Pattern standard deviation index, 57
Pediatric glaucoma. *See* Childhood glaucoma
Penetrating trauma, open-angle glaucoma and, 77, 78
Perimetry
  Armaly-Drance screening, 53–54, 53*i*
  automated static, 55
    artifacts seen on, 58–60
    high false-positive rate in, 60, 61*i*
    incorrect corrective lens used in, 60
    learning effect and, 60, 62*i*
  blue/yellow, 46
  clinical, 46–47
  definition of terms used in, 46–47
  in glaucoma, 44–65
    patterns of nerve loss and, 47, 48–52*i*
  interpretation in
    serial field, 60–65
    single field, 57–60
  kinetic, 46
  manual, 53–55
  screening, 56
    Armaly-Drance, 53–54, 53*i*
  static, 46
  suprathreshold, 46, 55
  threshold, 46, 55, 56, 56*i*, 57*i*
  threshold-related, 55
  variables in, 47–53
Perkins tonometer, 22
Persistent hyperplastic primary vitreous, angle-closure glaucoma and, 95
Phacoanaphylaxis, 76
Phacolytic glaucoma, 76
Phacomorphic glaucoma, 88
Phospholine. *See* Echothiophate
Photocoagulation, panretinal, acute angle-closure glaucoma after, 95
Photophobia, in infantile glaucoma, 98
PHPV. *See* Persistent hyperplastic primary vitreous
Physiologic cupping, glaucomatous cupping differentiated from, 41–42
Physostigmine, for glaucoma, 109*t*

Pigment dispersion syndrome, 74–75
    glaucoma and, 75
Pigmentary glaucoma, 74–75
Pilagan. *See* Pilocarpine
Pilocar. *See* Pilocarpine
Pilocarpine
    for acute angle closure, 84
    for glaucoma, 106–107, 107–110,
        108–109*t*
Plateau iris, 86, 87*i*
Plateau iris syndrome, 86, 88*i*
Pneumatic tonometer, 22
Portable electronic applanation tonometer,
    22
    infection control and, 24
Posner-Schlossman syndrome
    (glaucomatocyclitic crisis), 77
Posterior aqueous diversion syndrome. *See*
    Ciliary-block glaucoma
Posterior segment tumors, angle-closure
    glaucoma caused by, 91
Posttraumatic angle recession, 33, 37*i*,
    77, 78
Prader-Willi syndrome, childhood
    glaucoma and, 103*t*
Prelaminar layer of optic nerve head,
    36, 39*i*
Prematurity, retinopathy of, angle-closure
    glaucoma and, 95
Pressure gonioscopy (indentation/
    compression gonioscopy), 29, 30*i*, 32*i*
Primary angle-closure glaucoma
    acute, 83–84
    chronic, 85
    with pupillary block, 82–86
        epidemiology of, 82–83
        pathophysiology of, 83
    without pupillary block, 86, 87*i*, 88*i*
    subacute, 84
Primary open-angle glaucoma, 66–68
    clinical features of, 67
    disorders associated with, 67–68
    epidemiology of, 66
    hereditary and genetic factors in, 10, 66
Progressive iris atrophy, 91, 92*i*
Propine. *See* Dipivefrin
Prostaglandin analogs, 109*t*, 111
Pseudoexfoliation. *See* Exfoliation
    syndrome
Pseudophakia, pupillary block and, 88

Pupillary block
    mechanism of angle closure and,
        81, 82*i*
    in primary angle-closure glaucoma,
        82–86
        epidemiology of, 82–83
        pathophysiology of, 83
    in secondary angle-closure glaucoma,
        88–89
    previous pupillary block and, 89
Pupils
    dilation of, angle-closure glaucoma
        induced by, 85–86
    examination of, in glaucoma, 25–26
    and size affecting perimetry results,
        60, 64*i*

Refraction
    in glaucoma evaluation, 25
    low-vision management in glaucoma
        patients and, 129
Retinal detachment, nonrhegmatogenous,
    elevated intraocular pressure caused
    by, 89
Retinal nerve fiber distribution, 36, 38*i*
Retinal surgery, acute angle-closure
    glaucoma after, 94–95
Retinal vascular disease, acute angle-
    closure glaucoma after, 94–95
Retinal vein occlusion, central
    angle-closure glaucoma and, 95
    open-angle glaucoma and, 68
Retinopathy of prematurity, angle-closure
    glaucoma and, 95
Retrolaminar layer of optic nerve head,
    38, 39*i*
Retrolental fibroplasia. *See* Retinopathy of
    prematurity
Rubinstein-Taybi syndrome (broad thumb
    syndrome), childhood glaucoma
    and, 102*t*

Schiøtz tonometry (indentation tonometry),
    19, 22–23
    infection control and, 24
Schlemm's canal, 14
    aqueous outflow through, 14, 16
    gonioscopic visualization of, 33
Sclera, evaluation of in glaucoma, 26

Scleral buckling, acute angle-closure
  glaucoma after, 94–95
Sclerectomy
  full-thickness, for open-angle glaucoma,
    118, 120*i*
  operative considerations in, 121
Sclerostomy, laser and mechanical, for
  open-angle glaucoma, 122
Scotomata
  arcuate Bjerrum, in glaucoma, 47, 49*i*
  definition of, 47
  paracentral, in glaucoma, 47, 48*i*
Screening tests, in glaucoma, perimetry
  for, 55
  Armaly-Drance, 53–54, 53*i*
Secondary angle-closure glaucoma
  with pupillary block, 88–89
    previous pupillary block and, 89
  without pupillary block, 89–95
Secondary open-angle glaucoma, 72–80
  accidental injury and, 77–80
  drug use and, 80
  episcleral venous pressure increase
    and, 77
  exfoliation syndrome (pseudoexfoliation)
    and, 72–74
  intraocular tumors causing, 76
  lens-induced, 76
  ocular inflammation and, 76–77
  pigmentary, 74–75, 74*i*, 75
  surgical trauma causing, 77–80
Seidel test, in flat anterior chamber, 89
Senile sclerotic normal- (low-) tension
  glaucoma, 70
Shaffer system, for grading anterior
  chamber angle width, 32–33
Shocket shunt procedure, for open-angle
  glaucoma, 122
Sickle cell hemoglobinopathies, open-
  angle glaucoma and, 78, 79
Siderosis, open-angle glaucoma and, 78
Slit-lamp methods, for optic disc
  evaluation, 40
Sodium/potassium pump, in aqueous
  outflow, 15
Spaeth gonioscopic grading system,
  33, 34*i*
Splinter hemorrhages, in glaucoma, 43

Static perimetry, definition of, 46
Stickler syndrome (hereditary progressive
  arthro-ophthalmopathy), childhood
  glaucoma and, 102*t*
Suprathreshold, in perimetry
  definition of, 46
  testing, 55
Surgery, open-angle glaucoma associated
  with, 77–80
Synechiae, anterior
  chamber angle vessels in development
    of, 33
  iris processes differentiated from, 33, 35*i*

Television, closed-circuit, in low-vision
  management in glaucoma
  patients, 129
Temporal wedge defect, in glaucoma,
  47, 51*i*
Threshold, in perimetry, definition of, 46
Threshold-related screening strategy, in
  glaucoma, 55, 55*i*
Threshold testing, in glaucoma, 55, 56,
  56*i*, 57*i*
Thymoxamine, angle-closure risk
  minimized by, 86
Timolol, for glaucoma, 105, 108*t*
Timoptic. *See* Timolol
Tonography, 17
Tonometry (tonometer)
  applanation, 19–22
  Goldmann, 20–22
  infection control in, 24
  noncontact (air-puff), 22
  Perkins, 22
  pneumatic, 22
  portable, 22
  Schiøtz (indentation), 19, 22–23
Trabecular ablation, selective laser, for
  angle-closure glaucoma, 125
Trabecular meshwork, 14, 17*i*
  aqueous outflow through, 14, 16
  pigmentation of, 33
Trabeculectomy
  cataract extraction combined with,
    118–120
  for open-angle glaucoma, 118, 119*i*
Trabeculoplasty, laser, for open-angle
  glaucoma, 116–118

Trabeculopuncture, laser, for childhood glaucoma, 126
Trabeculotomy, for childhood glaucoma, 100, 125–126, 127*i*
Transscleral diode laser cyclophotocoagulation, for ciliary body ablation
  for childhood glaucoma, 127
  for open-angle glaucoma, 122
Transscleral Nd:YAG laser cyclophotocoagulation, for ciliary body ablation
  for childhood glaucoma, 127
  for open-angle glaucoma, 122
Trauma
  angle-closure glaucoma and, 94
  anterior chamber injury caused by, 33, 37*i*, 77, 78
  open-angle glaucoma and, 77–80
Trisomy 13 (Patau syndrome), childhood glaucoma and, 102*t*
Trisomy 18 (Edwards syndrome/trisomy E syndrome), childhood glaucoma and, 102*t*
Trisomy 21 (Down syndrome/trisomy G syndrome), childhood glaucoma and, 102*t*
Trusopt. *See* Dorzolamide
Tube-shunt surgery
  for angle-closure glaucoma, 125
  for open-angle glaucoma, 122
Tumors, intraocular. *See* Intraocular tumors
Turner syndrome, childhood glaucoma and, 102*t*

Ultrafiltration, in aqueous humor formation, 14

Ultrasound biomicroscopy
  in glaucoma, 26, 27*i*
  for plateau iris identification, 86, 87*i*
Uveal cysts, angle-closure glaucoma caused by, 91
Uveal melanomas, angle-closure glaucoma caused by, 91
Uveitis, in angle-closure glaucoma, 88
Uveoscleral outflow, 16

VEP. *See* Visual evoked potentials
Viral inflammation of eye, open-angle glaucoma and, 77
Visual evoked potentials, in glaucoma identification, 46
Visual field defects, in glaucoma, 7, 44–65. *See also specific type*
  low-vision aids and, 128
Visual field progression, in glaucoma, 60–65, 63*i*
Visual fields, in glaucoma, evaluation of, 44–65. *See also* Perimetry
Vitrectomy, for ciliary-block glaucoma, 125
Vitreous, persistent hyperplastic primary, angle-closure glaucoma and, 95
Vitreous surgery, pars plana, acute angle-closure glaucoma after, 94

Xalatan. *See* Latanoprost

Zeiss lens, for gonioscopy, 29, 30*i*
Zellweger syndrome (cerebrohepatorenal syndrome), childhood glaucoma and, 102*t*

ILLUSTRATIONS

The authors submitted the following figures for this revision:

Louis Cantor, MD: Fig VI-8, Fig VI-16

Elizabeth A. Hodapp, MD: Fig VI-14, Fig VI-15, Fig XI-1

M. Roy Wilson, MD: Fig VII-2, Fig VIII-3A, Fig VIII-3B